Character Education

*The
Birth of Hope
through
Unconditional Love
for
Total Fulfillment*

Virgie M. Binford
Rona Leach

Copyright 2002 by Virgie M. Binford and Rona Leach

All rights reserved. Written permission must be secured from the publisher to use or reproduce any part of this book, except for brief quotations in critical reviews or articles.

Printed in the United States of America

06   05   04   03   02   1   2   3   4   5

Library of Congress Catalog Card Number: 2002103365

ISBN: 1-57736-261-6

Cover design by Gary Bozeman

Photo of Virgie Binford by Dementi Studio, 121 E. Grace St., Richmond, VA 23219.

Photo of Rona Leach by Olan Mills, Inc.

238 Seaboard Lane • Franklin, Tennessee 37067
800-321-5692
www.providencepubcorp.com

CONTENTS

DEDICATION		vi
INTRODUCTION		vii
C	1. Change When Necessary for Improvements	1
H	2. Hope in Generating Possibilities to Succeed	6
A	3. Accept the Best in Self and the Rest	10
R	4. Reserve and Restore Faith in Systems that Work	15
A	5. Apply Problem-Solving Techniques	18
C	6. Commit to Achieving Excellence	21
T	7. Teach and Learn	25
E	8. Energize Self and Exercise Support of Others	29
R	9. Reward Success	34
E	10. Engage in Two-Way Conversation	37
D	11. Deepen the Well of Security	40
U	12. Understand Rules for Acceptable Behavior	43
C	13. Communicate on a Two-Way Basis	49
A	14. Admit Mistakes and Improve	52
T	15. Think Before You Speak	55
I	16. Interact for Positive Outcomes	58
O	17. Open Doors to Diversity	61
N	18. Nurture Success in the Journey of Life	63
EPILOGUE		67
NOTES		68
BIBLIOGRAPHY		70
ABOUT THE AUTHORS		72

TO MY YOUNGEST SISTER, Margaret Elaine Mattic, a victim of the terrorist attack at the World Trade Center on September 11, 2001. With flawless character, a caring, concerned, and positive mental attitude and a demonstration of unconditional love and respect for all mankind, she strived to set and achieve goals that resulted in moral excellence and brought out the best in mind, body, and soul.

It is my prayer that her life was not lost in vain and that her devotion to character education will serve as a road map for enhancing peace on earth and goodwill for all inhabitants.

Hopefully, readers of this book will increase their knowledge, skills, and creative strategies to make character education an integral part of the teaching-learning process.

Forever,
V. M. Binford

I AM DEEPLY HONORED to dedicate this book to my parents, the late Ranzie and Sarah Leach, who raised me in a nurturing environment of love, care, compassion, obedience, and respect. It was indeed through my upbringing by my parents that I learned firsthand what "character" was all about.

They taught me early on the difference between right and wrong, lived decently and honorably in my presence, and practiced many character traits which are emphasized in this book. Their unconditional love, guidance, and patience have helped me to go down this road of life and really appreciate the gift they shared with me.

Ranzie and Sarah did not know *in name* anything about character-building, but both of them embraced to the fullest those traits which bond a family together. I will forever be indebted to them for the sacrifices they made to make sure I was well cared for and loved unconditionally. My goal is to continue to live a life that I know would make both of them proud of their daughter, their only child, their Rona.

I will always love you,
Rona

INTRODUCTION

 Good character accounts for the ability to master integrity by discerning right from wrong and also to the inner-winning spirit's ability to overcome obstacles of defective personality in order to succeed in spite of odds. Character education is training mind, body, and soul to overcome inadequacies and to develop resilience in order to conquer destructive behavior.

We have recorded evidences of the positive results of character education on a generation of fragmented personalities. After years of training and research, we witnessed firsthand the birth of desirable behaviors from poorly behaved persons after they experienced our program of care, concern, and commitment.

We aim to facilitate hope in the hopeless, to foster *I can* attitudes in the *I cant's*, to encourage positive behavior instead of negative reactions, and to promote goal setting and decision making to replace low self-esteem and careless existence. Planting these seeds through character education will harvest overpowering solutions in a society that faces many challenges.

Believing in the axiom "where there is a will there is a way" fired our enthusiasm to write this publication. Our vision is to kindle the flame of hope, faith, and unconditional love for character education as a tool for enhancing excellence in daily living.

Names of characters cited in this book have been changed to protect the privacy of those who have battled to survive adversity.

This volume is a blueprint for chartering an inner-winning course that will make life's journey peaceful, joyful, and profitable. It will help you overcome obstacles and turn them into opportunities to find needs and fill them. Throughout the book there are specific instructions for home, school, and community activities that will help you enhance positive attributes and will empower your family to cope with life's many challanges.

Research, practical applications, home-learning activities, and enrichment materials are combined to make this publication a teaching and learning tool for children and families.

Chapter One

Change When Necessary for Improvements

Often, communication among family members and others follows predetermined rules and regulations. Participants in the group may affirm: "This is the way it has always been done, so why change?" We believe that if something has been prescribed that is incorrect, repetition will not make it right. Recalling the words of one unknown writer confirms our view, "There are three sides to any issue—your side, my side, and the right side." So it appears that change is inevitable when it is necessary.

In his publication *Winning the Brain Race*, David Kearns outlines a six-point Education Recovery Plan:

- Choice
- Restructuring
- Professionalism
- Standards
- Values
- Federal responsibility[1]

Marva Collins, the founder of Westside Preparatory School for grades one through nine, stresses the importance of change in outmoded systems of education and excellence in teaching and learning. She emphasizes that "for almost every ill in our society, we can realistically point back to a loss of values . . . such as determination, perseverance, keeping your word, honesty and integrity. . . ." To clarify her point of view that change is necessary in education, she insists that "America cannot produce literate, thinking leaders of society by reading such bandits as *See Sue, See Dick, See Jane. . . .* We must once again give our children substance in stories that deal with steadfastness and determination."[2]

Many authors agree with Celia Decker, who defines character education in *Children in Early Years*. She proclaimed that, "Character is an inward force that guides a person's conduct. It helps people make choices that meet acceptable standards of right and wrong."[3]

Initiating exemplary qualities in character education is the responsibility of parents and guardians in the home. Developing character is not a ready-made pattern of operation, but is a continuously evolving practice of goal setting, decision making, and role modeling. The process is made up of the stepping stones of wise choices, knowledge, skills, and creativity which result in integrity, honesty, wisdom, self-confidence, and self-worth. An explanation by Sue Spayh Riley in *How to Generate Values in Young Children* declares that acceptable values must be "searched out, tried out, discussed, and analyzed." In her discussion of the growth and development of young children, Riley states, "When we stand back and give children time to explore, to discover their own answers, to search for the answers even if they do not find them—there is learning in the search—we are providing five stretches of open road for growth and decision making."[4]

Emphasizing that parents are the first teachers of morality, Richard Sterns says that "our moral behavior is based on choice, knowledge, and understanding of what our goals are. . . . The moral code you develop will affect the choices you make every day. . . . They will affect how you conduct yourself in school and the workplace and they will affect the way you behave as a citizen of your town, state, and country."

Charles Schafer shared these ten guidelines for helping children set goals for self-improvement in his book, *How to Influence Children: A Complete Guide for Becoming a Better Parent*:

- Be specific
- Keep score
- Set reasonable goals
- Break down big goals
- Watch your timing
- Involve the child
- Establish a deadline
- Review periodically
- Reinforce achievement
- Turn complaints into specific goals.[5]

This publication outlines the role of parents and caretakers in helping children thrive and succeed in self-improvement. Specifically, we give dependable procedures that will help you be predictable, orderly, and supportive as you shape your child's character.

Each chapter in this publication has suggested home learning activities that will foster family interaction. They are designed to help you include character education as you plan, implement, and assess daily activities.

Based on the format developed by Ira J. Gordon and Associates that was nationally validated for replication as a Parent Education Model in 1977, each activity includes:

- Title of activity
- Purpose of activity
- List of teaching tools that are needed
- Description of how the activity will be conducted
- Exploration of other ways to enrich the activity

We hope you'll enjoy using these practical activities as you embark on your journey of character education.

HOME LEARNING ACTIVITY

HOME AND FAMILY

1. These are things that make me happy about my home and family:

   _____
   _____
   _____

2. These are some things I would like to change:

   _____
   _____
   _____

3. These are things I love about me:

   _____
   _____
   _____

4. These are things I wish I could change to make me a better person:

   _____
   _____
   _____

5. This is my favorite picture:

Change When Necessary for Improvements

ENRICHMENT ACTIVITY

"Kokomo, Don't Mess with that Bumblebee!"
An *original poem* by Rona Leach

Suggestion: Read the poem, discuss, and react to it.
Draw or cut out a picture to illustrate it.
Have fun!

"Kokomo, Don't Mess with that Bumblebee!"

Mrs. Hattie had a big old cat
Whose name was Kokomo.
He pranced around on four black paws,
But his coat was as white as snow.

Now Kokomo had a mind of his own,
No one could tell him a thing.
He'd set on the back porch with Mrs. Hat,
While she would crochet, knit, and sing.

This big old cat was full of mischief,
Spending his time looking for things to distract,
He'd unravel her thread and knock over the bread
And watch how Mrs. Hat would react.

He'd catch the clothes on the line
And pull them to the ground.
And pull the flowers from the pots
Then make a playful sound.

This cat just loved to chase live things,
And roll over in the grass.
And catch Mrs. Hattie's apron string
As she would walk right past.

One summer's day while Kokomo
Lay sleeping in the weeds,
A great big bumblebee appeared
And landed on his knees.

Mrs. Hat looked up from her back porch
And saw the look on her cat's face.
She knew this bee and Kokomo,
Would be in for a race.

"Now listen to me Kokomo,
Leave that bumblebee alone!
Just let him go on 'bout his way
And you come right on home."

By now I'm sure you know the rest,
Kokomo did not obey.
He jumped right up and snapped his teeth
So the bee could fly away.

Mrs. Hat stood up and raised her voice.
"Now Kokomo, you quit!
Don't bother with that bumblebee,
And stop right now, that's it!"

But Kokomo tried one more time
To bite the bumblebee.
He raised his head and opened his mouth,
And closed his mouth, you see.

The bumblebee went right on in
And landed on Kokomo's tongue.
The bumblebee just gave a sting
That made Kokomo want to run.

The look on Kokomo's shocked face,
Was a sight you wouldn't believe.
He grinned, and stretched, and blinked, and frowned,
But the pain he could not relieve.

He tried to spit out the bumblebee,
But to his mouth, he stuck.
Kokomo went running to Mrs. Hat,
To get him out of this rut.

"I tried to tell you Kokomo,
To leave that bee alone.
Now here you are with one big mouth,
That you will bring back home.

"I hope that you now understand,
When I talk to you in this tone.
And really truly understand,
To leave bumblebees alone."

Chapter Two

Hope in Generating Possibilities to Succeed

 Oftentimes, schools are the focus of discussion on program development and implementation. Of course, this is commendable and noteworthy. But often, educators, parents, and community leaders overlook or underestimate the power of the family structure. Children spend an enormous amount of time in the home during their first four years of life. The family has a wonderful opportunity to mold and cultivate a child's ability to make correct choices between right and wrong. Within this framework lies hope in generating possibilities to succeed.

During their formative years, children are constantly observing, mimicking, and doing as they see others do. Within these years lie enormous opportunities to teach, model, and provide wonderful and exciting dialogue on the correct versus the incorrect way to behave. Where is a better place to plant the seed of hope than at home around the family? You have the excellent opportunity as parents to put in place your own family-tailored character education program. Every family member plays a major role and is a primary character in this special program. What other place would be better to learn about honesty, respect, responsibility, fairness, loyalty, trustworthiness, caring, sharing, and other character traits than in your home with your children?

The home is where hope in generating possibilities to succeed originates and grows. If the home nests an atmosphere of hopelessness, the possibility for success for children will be difficult. Homemade character education programs can be integrated into every aspect of family life when everyone in the home is actively involved and is held accountable for their actions.

Sharing and caring home environments are created when every member in the household is held accountable and each accepts responsibility for her actions. The focus must be aimed at the success, safety, happiness, and well-being of each family member. Even though a child is only a toddler, he is still capable of understanding the safety aspects of his home. This understanding keeps him safe, and keeps his family happy and more secure about his well-being. One is never too young nor too old to be an active participant in a site-based homemade character cducation program.

As parents, you have the first chance to develop and put in place a successful, enjoyable, and nurturing homemade character program which can make a positive difference in your family. Other families in your community, state, and nation can replicate your program. It is our hope that your family character education program will be a living and ongoing project which will help enhance family life, the benefits of which will extend to many generations to come. As your children live and grow, so will this delightful homemade character program.

What a wonderful contribution you can give to your children as well as those who are born many years down the road. How many of us were taught many years ago ways of accomplishing a task in our home and do likewise with our families? We treasure those gifts by not only doing as we were taught to do, but also by teaching it to our family members. Just think of what a positive impact each family member can have on contributing to the growth of the family, the community, and the world. With your homemade character education program in place, you are truly providing hope in generating possibilities to succeed.

Before finding possible solutions to problems such as lack of respect, not assuming responsibilities, an attitude of non-caring, and violence among youth, it is important to try and research and determine why they behave this way. Dr. James E. Shaw, the author of *Jack and Jill, Why They Kill: Saving Our Children, Saving Ourselves* attempts to get to the root of the why behind many of the violent actions recently committed. His detailed case studies of thirteen youth who committed violent acts is an eye-opener to each of us, and he lets us know that each of us has a responsibility to start first with our homes. Shaw's explanation of why he wrote this book with possible solutions brings to light a frightening fact. He indicated in his account that we are "losing the equivalent of a classroom of children every forty-eight hours to acts of homicide."[6] His ideas revolve around the question, "What can parents and teachers do to restore peace and sanity to our homes and schools?"

Through his years of research with 103 youth, thirteen documented case studies, and hours of interviewing youth shines a ray of hope in generating possibilities to succeed. But of course, the ultimate objective is to prevent acts of violence from occurring in the first place. One of our greatest resources for providing remedies is within the home environment. Instilling in children early on the ability to discern the difference between right and wrong is vital in generating possibilities for success.

The Association For Supervision and Curriculum Development Spring 2001 Curriculum Update provided a very strong article speaking to the importance of hope in generating possibilities to succeed in the article, "Learning on the Home Front," by Amy Eckman. "All parents are teachers, but not all parents appreciate the tremendous influence that the home learning environment has on their child's potential for intellectual and social success."[7] This brings to mind not only the development of the academic aspect of a child's life, but also how a child can cope and get along with others. After they had committed violent acts, many children said in interviews that they could not get along with family members or they could not get along with their peers. So often, they lacked the skills of handling themselves appropriately in situations of conflict. If this is the case, as adults what are we failing to do to help our children cope with the inevitable failures and heartbreaks they encounter throughout their lives? Are we teaching them only about succeeding? Should we not also teach them that failure is a part of life, and we must use that failure to generate possibilities for success?

Let's go into a child's mind as we remember the story about the tortoise and the hare. This is a delightful children's story, written long ago, which teaches each of us about perseverance, never giving up, and sticking to it. Of course, it was the nature of the tortoise to be slow, but so what? He was slow, but he persevered. There was something inside of him. Perhaps it was genetics or maybe at an early age his parents instilled in him a stick-to-it-no-matter-what attitude. Maybe they taught him that even if he didn't get there first, he would still get there! With this very minute belief, hope in generating possibilities to succeed was ingrained. What a lovely gift to give to a child.

William J. Bennett, in *The Book of Virtues*, expounds very clearly on this trait. "How do we encourage our children to persevere, to persist in their efforts to improve themselves, their own lot, and the lot of others? By standing by them, and with them, and behind them; by being coaches and cheerleaders; and by the witness of our own examples."[8]

Dr. Helen R. LeGette, another noted scholar in the area of character education, has outlined twenty-one factors which help pave the way in the home in implementing successful character education projects. Dr. LeGette's resource *Parents, Kids and Character: 21 Strategies to Help Your Child Develop Good Character* clearly speaks to showing children proper actions through active involvement. "Model good character in the home," is first and foremost on her list.[9] She further details the importance of modeling good character in the home by eluding to a statement by William Bennett from his book, *The Book of Virtues*: "There is nothing more influential, more determinant in a child's life than the moral power of a quiet example. It is critically important that those who are attempting to influence children's character in positive ways walk the talk."[10] This points again to the importance of the parents' role in making sure that good character is taught and is a part of everyday home activities.

The goal of this parents' manual is to simply give you some facts, to provide the opportunity for you to begin thinking about what you and your family would like to do to enhance character in your home, and to give you a framework. With this in place, you will then have the task of designing and tailoring your family project which will be unique and enjoyable for all involved. By now, you are probably wondering what character traits you will target as a part of your family activity. That is a decision that you and your family must make. Once everyone knows about the homemade family project and the character goals are in place, it will become a project by which you will learn and will enjoy together as a family.

Through research and reading, you will learn that there are many character traits. The Character Counts Coalition has developed what are called the six pillars of character: respect, trustworthiness, responsibility, caring, fairness, and citizenship. These six pillars of character came about as a result of a 1992 survey released by the Josephson Institute of Ethics. By no means are these all of the character traits. Again, you may work to focus on concerns that you and your family have in your home. Are all family members completing their chores? Do all family members cooperate when there are things to be done? If we fail, do we continue to work at it? If things don't go our way, can we change? Again, these questions give rise to other character traits that may interest you and your family such as: loyalty, cooperation, perseverance, or flexibility. These are just a few other character traits which may interest you.

The objective at this point is to provide an opportunity for you and your family to start talking and shaping your homemade character program. This should be a project by which all family members claim ownership and work together to make it happen. It should make you stronger as individuals and as a family. Children should be able to learn at home and carry these traits to school where they will be able to successfully cope and become strong and independent individuals while respecting themselves and others.

The next page consists of one of your first family-oriented activities. Please take time together to develop your direction for your homemade character program. The depth of your brainstorming, the level of involvement from all family members, and understanding the role of each family member remains crucial in the success of your program. So, get the family together, brainstorm, outline, and design your program.

FAMILY IDEAS

A Few Relevant Questions

1. Do we want to work on a character program plan together as a family?

_____
_____
_____
_____

2. What are our ideas for a character education program?

_____
_____
_____
_____

3. What character traits would we like to learn about and integrate into our family activities?

_____
_____
_____
_____

4. What will be the role of each family member?

_____
_____
_____
_____

Name of our family program:

_____

Example: The Leach's Rapping and Rocking Character Plan (LRRCP)

Hope in Generating Possibilities to Succeed

Chapter Three

Accept the Best in Self and the Rest

One of the strongest factors in developing good character is self-respect. Close your eyes and visualize a world where every human being respects herself. This alone would change the world for the better. Many of the problems we now encounter would cease to exist or at least would be minimized. Conflicts among human beings would be fewer in number. People would be more likely to talk to each other, discuss their genuine concerns, listen to the other side, and reach reasonable solutions. Can you envision a world with less crime, more open communication, and a much better understanding and appreciation for the existence of others?

Is this possible? Why not? Each of us has an opportunity to plant the seed of self-respect first in ourselves and to cultivate it daily. It has the potential to grow within us and spread its roots to others around us. Self-respect, just as any other term, may mean different things to different people. What is your idea of the meaning of self-respect? Well, let's look at a likely definition. Self-respect means the ability for one to believe and act in such a manner that it is productive and beneficial to oneself as well as others. Again, parents are the planters of the seeds of self-respect.

Dr. Shaw discusses in his book *Jack and Jill, Why They Kill* the factor of moral intelligence and the role parents play in ensuring that moral intelligence is a part of home life. "It is vital that parents ensure that their own children grow up free of the shackles of stereotyped ideas and prejudices—ideas that fuel racism, sexism, religionism, alienation and social discomfort—and learn to respect and interact with others, regardless of their race, creed, religion or lifestyle preference. Such respect is an invaluable asset. . . ."[11]

Just as respect helps to bring about better world relations, so it brings about a much better and warmer home environment. Various organizations, groups, and systems have embarked upon integrating character traits into their daily operations. Research has revealed that respect is a predominant character trait in most programs that have been studied.

One beneficial feature about gaining self-respect is that it transcends the self and allows one to respect others. If a level of respect is prevalent in a home among all family members, it can give rise to a much happier and wholesome home environment. If it is possible for respect to surpass the self and overflow into the lives of other family members, is it not also possible for respect to spill over from home to school to the community?

At this point, perhaps you are thinking of ways to foster respect in your home. Again, this is an activity in which everyone can participate. It gives the adults in the family an opportunity to assume the primary role in the enhancement of respect through your homemade character program. Dr. LeGette's *Parents, Kids and Character: 21 Strategies to Help Your Child Develop Good Character*, details in the following quote the important role parents play in ensuring that respect is a part of everyday activities. "Show respect for your spouse, your children, and other family members.... If children experience respect firsthand within the family, they are more likely to be respectful of others. Simply stated, respect begets respect."[12]

The beauty about designing and putting your homemade character program in place is that it sets the stage for family conversation, creativity, and the opportunity for everyone to become involved. It is easily integrated into the varied daily activities. Getting along together makes life so much easier. Perhaps one of the greatest values of a family-designed program is knowing that everyone is accountable for creating a peaceful and enjoyable home life. Experiencing a stressful day on the job or at school is more the reason for getting a wonderful stress-relieving program off the ground and in place at home. It is important for home to be a place where you enjoy talking, laughing, and exchanging conversation with family members. Home can be a refuge from the hustle and bustle of life's fast-paced activities. It should be comprised of an atmosphere with little to no confusion. Any environment will have its problems, but home should serve as a place where problems can be openly discussed and managed in such a way that it will benefit everyone in the household.

By now you are bubbling over with ideas of how to implement these traits. An excellent starting point can be looking at your daily activities together as a family. Let's think together! What is a typical weekday like in your home starting with the early morning hours? Is everyone up at the same time, moving at the same time, or are you all moving up and down, in and out at various times? What are some things that each family member could do to respect the necessary activities of other family members? Again, we are speaking of the need for each family member to do his part. Remember, "respect begets respect."

Okay, let's document what we do and how we can change to help other family members experience a more peaceful home setting. Included in this chapter is a sample chart which can be used to begin your documentation on any character trait your family deems appropriate and needs immediate action to make the home a happier dwelling. Look at the chart, call a family meeting, and discuss openly and in a peaceful manner your course of action for each member. By so doing, you are expressing needs by being honest and up front with each other. You will probably discover that some of the things you do on a daily basis have a negative impact on other family members. If so, discovering this is a very positive move. An awareness of yourself and making small changes can make a world of difference as you strive to bring more peace and harmony into your home. Now, please review the sample chart and the activity which follows it.

Sample Family Character Program

What am I doing and how can I change to better my family?

Character trait: *respect*   Time: *early morning*   Date documented: *February 1, 2002*

Family member: *Things I do:*   *Improvements for self and family:*

Mom   Get up at 5:30 A.M and turn on all lights.   Select only several lights to turn on in the mornings, away from the family

Roll my hair in the early morning.   Take time to set hair at night.

_____   _____   _____

Family Character Program

What am I doing and how can I change to better my family?

Character trait: _____   Time: _____   Date documented: _____

Family member: *Things I do:*   *Improvements for self and family:*

_____   _____   _____

HOME LEARNING ACTIVITY

HAVE I IMPROVED?

Use on a periodic basis to monitor your individual progress.
Discuss with your family members.

Character trait: _____
Date: _____
Family member: _____

* _____
_____
_____

Character trait: _____
Date: _____
Family member: _____

* _____
_____
_____

Character trait: _____
Date: _____
Family member: _____

* _____
_____
_____

Character trait: _____
Date: _____
Family member: _____

* _____
_____
_____

Other comments: _____
_____
_____
_____
_____

This activity may be slightly difficult for everyone. You must become comfortable discussing your strengths and weaknesses with your family members. You probably discussed concerns of other family members of which you were unaware. If so, that is wonderful, and you are on your way to charting a productive homemade family character program. If your purpose is to strive to make a stronger family, you must be honest with each other and willing to discuss concerns. How can we become more respectful of each other in our home? It could be something as simple as getting up in the morning, not turning on the main light, but turning on a small lamp which will be less disturbing to other family members.

The sample chart will assist you in working through concerns of each family member and providing a means by which to monitor improvement. You could approach this in a number of ways. You may decide to come together as a family and discuss on a weekly or monthly basis. When you convene for discussion, have family members bring their list to the family character rap session. Make it a family gathering with cookies, milk, or even pizza! This time together is not only for revisiting what you have done, but it could be an hour of getting together, talking, laughing, and celebrating each other's successes. Bring the baby to the meeting! As parents and children grow and learn together, so will the little one(s). They will experience the joy of family bonding and respect.

It is left up to the family to decide the length of time during the year you devote to a particular character trait. If by chance family members observe the demise of a selected trait, you may revisit it to remind each other of your commitments. Respect is a wonderful (timely) trait to start off with during the month of January. If you start the year off by respecting self and your other family members, other traits such as orderliness, kindness, responsibility, caring, trustworthiness, honesty, cooperation, and sincerity will fall in place within the walls of your home. Projects such as this would work well in the development of an entire community character program. Remember, you are empowered as a family to design your unique program. Persevere!

Chapter Four

Reserve and Restore Faith in Systems that Work

 I often reflect on the importance of reserving and restoring faith in systems that work. A Girl Scouts' song that has been passed on for generations illustrates this idea in these words: "Make new friends but keep the old, one is silver and the other is gold." This song demonstrates the importance of replicating positive practices. Another popular song that embraces this point of view is: "You have to accentuate the positive and eliminate the negative." These words describe the need to promote systems that work.

Research reported by Dr. James Comer in his *School Development Program* that was initiated in 1968 validated restoring faith in systems that work. The main character in his research was his mother, who reserved and restored faith in systems that worked by sharing ways to enrich the teaching and learning process through the effective child development practices she used with her four children. Positive guidance and positive reinforcement resulted in them collectively earning thirteen academic degrees. Comer's publication, *Maggie's American Dream*, portrayed the central figure, his mother, as a person who promoted systems that worked. According to Comer, Maggie's contributions in the enhancement of excellence in education inspired thousands to elevate themselves from despair and failure to success in school and in life. The key element was parental involvement which produced excellence in education. With unity of purpose, home and school can make concerted efforts to turn around the schools where their children are trapped by circumstances.[13]

Character education has its origin in parent education and involvement that passed acceptable practices on to succeeding generations. Spin-off benefits of parental involvement are success in home, school, and community.

Individuals and groups have collaborated and cooperated in reserving and restoring faith in systems that work through various mentorship programs. Thomas Evans (1992), shared evidences of systems that work in his publication *Making a Difference in the Public Schools*. While working as an attorney in a law firm on Wall Street and serving as chairman of the board of teachers college at Columbia University, he founded Mentor, a program in which members of over five hundred law firms in twenty states have taken on the responsibility of working with students to bring out the best in them. These mentors made concerted efforts to establish bonds of support and positive reinforcement resulting in excellence through educational inspiration.

Evans's research reported positive outcomes of mentors whose efforts ignited flames of hope in hopeless situations. They shared faith, hope, and unconditional love with students who were falling through cracks of failure and appeared to be doomed as outcasts in a society that treated them as low self-esteemers in a wilderness of despair.

This book cites contributions of mentors from diversified backgrounds and financial status who used their knowledge, skills, and creativity to help others achieve maximum potential in all areas of life. Among those mentioned as positive role models is Eugene Lang whose success was developed when his college expenses were paid by a mentor. He probably would have remained in his career as a dishwasher in a local restaurant had he not been assisted financially. Lang remembered this act of kindness that had been bestowed on him by becoming a mentor to others. He utilized his competencies to make millions of dollars; and he has given away millions in the business of mentoring to the less fortunate. He launched a major support system for sixth graders in his former school in East Harlem, New York. As an invited speaker to the group, he promised them that if they would stay in school, he would finance their college education. He kept his promise.

Another faith restorer is Marva Collins who started Chicago's Westside Preparatory School in which she provided comprehensive programs for grades one through nine for needy students. She opened her school with five thousand dollars she withdrew from a pension fund that she earned while she was employed as a teacher in an inner city school. Through the support of her husband, she was successful in providing quality education for children that included teaching them classics. She stressed values, determination, perseverance, honesty, and integrity.

Other mentors in education include Bill and Camille Cosby. In an effort to develop well-rounded students, they contributed millions of dollars to enhance excellence in education. An example of their generosity was a gift of twenty million dollars they gave to Spellman College in 1988.

Pathfinders in this publication are in agreement that enhancement of excellence in education usually starts on a small scale. We make a difference by working with students and involving parents and other caretakers in the task of reserving and restoring faith in systems that work.

The outcome of character education was described by U.S. Senator John McCain in a commencement speech he made at Virginia Military Institute on May 19, 2001. In his address, as reported in the *Richmond Times Dispatch*, he stated: "It takes character to choose wisely and to serve well, and a sense of honor is the essence of all good character."[14]

Building character begins in the home with parents or other caretakers teaching by example. They must model desirable behavior, for children will imitate their actions. They must demonstrate the importance of being inner-winners in life by providing an adequate diet of character-building with continuous servings of honesty, responsibility, trust, and unconditional love.

Walking the walk exceeds talking the talk in importance when it comes to character education. When adults demonstrate exemplary character as role models, generations following will learn to replicate acceptable practices.

The following guidelines are "starter-uppers" for involvement of the family in making character-building an integral part of daily living:

HOME LEARNING ACTIVITY

1. What are some things you can do to show that you are caring, concerned, and committed to being a good helper at home, at school, in the workplace, and in the community?

2. Why is it important to volunteer to help those who are less fortunate?

3. What will you do to demonstrate that you have good behavior?

4. Share at least five activities that you believe demonstrate that character education is necessary for success in life.

5. List at least three things you learned from reading this chapter.

6. Share additional ideas that will be helpful for reserving and restoring faith in systems that work.

Chapter Five

Apply Problem-Solving Techniques

You are now on the way to establishing your homemade character program. The first four chapters have provided you with a general format as well as documented research on the positive impact of strong parental involvement in the home. The focus thus far has been to make you more aware of creating a more comfortable home environment for all family members. Once an awareness has been established, your family can begin to implement problem-solving techniques.

It is important to identify problems, accept that they exist, and apply strategies to help your family solve them. Just as larger and more complex organizations encounter challenges, so do families. One of the greatest assets in problem-solving is an open line of communication. Once a problem has been identified, forge forward by getting all family members involved in reaching possible solutions.

Communication in a home can open the door to the implementation of a number of character traits. Caring, flexibility, respect, fairness, cooperation, and honesty are just a few traits which are produced when family members talk with each other and share their feelings about the home environment. Look at the problems that could be solved if we took time to talk to each other and listen to each other's points of view. Hearing and understanding the other side of the story can provide so much insight.

Talking about concerns leads to a fruitful ending if everyone is focused on creating a comfortable home setting. You can come together around the table on a weekly or biweekly basis and just talk. You may have very little control with what goes on at the job site or at school, but each family member has influence in shaping the daily and weekly activities in the home. This communication helps to establish ownership in the home.

Let's look at a family chat session. One family member should be instrumental in getting the family together for at least one hour each week. Inform all family members that the discussion will center around several challenges the family is facing. Everyone's opinions will be heard at this meeting. The entire family will agree on one specific challenge that they want to apply problem-solving techniques. Quite often the solution to one challenge may minimize other problems. A sample form follows for you to use to document the challenge, to map out possible solutions, to assign responsibilities to family members, and to establish a time line for updates. This is a wonderful problem-solving family activity.

Once you convene and discuss each member's possible solution to the challenge, you may discover that one family member alone may not offer the best solution. Solutions may come from a combination of several thoughts, ideas, and suggestions. You may also discover an untapped level of creativity which can nurture a delightful and happier family. It is perfectly okay if you meet together with family members, discuss the problems at hand, and discover solutions to other problems. Again, communicating with each other can be very productive and bonding for all involved. You may find it helpful to post the following worksheet on a bulletin board for all to see.

This activity should spark lots of conversation. It is also advisable to post the findings in an area of high visibility, where it can be periodically read by each family member. This will serve as a method of reinforcement and also a reminder to everyone. You may have children who are unable to read. If so, read this information to them and discuss it so they will know what it means. This will make them feel that they too are participating family members.

The bonding accomplished when family members explore solutions together creates trust and respect for one another. It also paves the way for suggestions and ideas that may be different, unique, and manageable for all involved. Caring and concern become basic ingredients in keeping everyone happy and safe when all are made to feel that they are a part of the solution.

Problems frequently allow everyone to *feel the pain*. When that is the case, solicit possible solutions from those in the family who experience pain so that a solution will allow everyone to *share the gain*.

Life comes with many challenges. Some may be unapproachable. Others can be dealt with through problem-solving techniques. If this practice is put in place in the home, discussed, and nurtured, life can be experienced at a greater level of fulfillment. Here lies the basic purpose behind chapter five—to activate, motivate, and heighten your family's level of problem-solving through awareness, communication, creativity, and flexibility.

Family Problem-Solving Worksheets

Our family challenges:
_____
_____

Possible solutions and assigned responsibilites:
_____
_____

First update:
Date:_____

Solution 1:_____
_____

Solution 2:_____
_____

Solution 3:_____
_____

Our family challenges:
_____
_____

Possible solutions and assigned responsibilities:
_____
_____

Second update:
Date:_____

Solution 1:_____
_____

Solution 2:_____
_____

Solution 3:_____
_____

Final family comments:
_____
_____

Chapter Six

COMMIT TO ACHIEVING EXCELLENCE

Excellence is a virtue that stems from developing maximum potential to achieve desired goals. It overcomes adversities and obstacles in life, resulting in exemplary status of nobility. It is a continuous process that results in bettering your best through goal setting and decision making.

William Menninger details six essential qualities in the pursuit of excellence:

- Sincerity
- Personal Integrity
- Humility
- Courtesy
- Wisdom
- Charity

William Menninger shares a prescription that enhances a commitment to excellence that mandates one to "find a mission and take it seriously."[15] This idea is expounded upon by Charles Garfield in his publication *Peak Performers: The New Heroes of American Business*. He describes people at their best as those that possess these qualities:

- Missions that motivate
- Results in real time
- Self-management through self-mastery
- Team building/team playing
- Course correction
- Change management[16]

John W. Gardner states, "Whoever I am or whatever I am doing, some kind of excellence is within my reach."[17] In order to fulfill dreams, desires, and commitments, one must take advantage of every opportunity. Maximum use must be made of human and natural resources. It does not mean that one must be loaded with the potential for excellence, but one must be committed to achieving what critics might call *impossible*.

Frank Lloyd Wright encouraged excellence with his affirmation: "Man built most nobly when limitations were the greatest."[18]

The following points will guide you on the path to excellence:

C Cultivate an attitude of care and concern. And commit to achieving your maximum potential.

O Open your mind and visualize continuous success.

M Make a plan and implement it.

M Manage material and spiritual resources of the body, mind, and soul to reap outcomes of excellence.

I Influence others to join in the search of excellence in the home, at school, and in the workplace.

T Teach basic skills for survival.

T Trust in your Creator to guide you in goal setting and decision making.

O Organize your schedule and set priorities to achieve your maximum potential.

A Aspire to reach higher than you expect.

C Choose mentors and establish a support system for continuous growth.

H Help others to succeed.

I Imagine the outcome of successfully completing desired goals.

E Energize yourself with daily positive affirmations.

V Value challenges for improvement as well as successes.

I Improve daily performances.

N Nurture character-building through decision making, dedication, honesty, integrity, and interpersonal relations.

G Give freely as a volunteer, finding needs and filling them.

E   Expect the best from yourself.

X   X-ray your mind to discover your strengths.

C   Communicate effectively on a two-way basis.

E   Enjoy the beauty in people, places, and things.

L   Love all people unconditionally.

L   Learn something new everyday.

E   Encourage the downtrodden to look up and live an enriched life.

N   Note your efforts and achievements in a daily journal.

C   Compliment others for a job well done or for steps taken in the right direction.

E   Enrich your life with spiritual gifts of faith, hope, and love.

The road to excellence takes hard work, strong determination, and persistence in climbing the ladder of success. It is undaunted faith, positive actions, and unconditional love for a voyage of unspeakable joy which will benefit society.

When you commit to excellence, the fire of determination will enable you to move out of the trenches of doubt and on to the highway of self-motivation. You will reach the finish line and experience satisfaction in being an inner-winner.

Utilizing these guidelines will empower you to harvest character by weeding out feelings of self-pity, doubt, and negative actions. You will replace them with acts of service by sharing good deeds, by trusting in your Higher Power, and by acting without expecting favors in return.

HOME LEARNING ACTIVITY

1. Discuss the definition of excellence and share at least five things you can do to achieve success as a family.

_____
_____
_____
_____

2. Share what you can do at school and at home to demonstrate that you understand the power of excellence for success in all activities.

_____
_____
_____
_____

3. List things that can be done in the community that will bring peace, happiness, and success for all people.

_____
_____
_____
_____

Chapter Seven

TEACH AND LEARN

 In order to be a competent teacher, one must have sufficient knowledge and creativity. An interest in learning will motivate you to think clearly, act responsibly, and pursue your studies. These attributes will enhance the quality of your education. To learn is to acquire knowledge, understanding, and skills for making discoveries. An active learner will make an excellent teacher.

"Teach and learn" are connectors which build faith, hope, and unconditional love. The learning process draws out the best in us physically, mentally, emotionally, and spiritually as we become mature thinkers and pursue self-fulfillment.

An effective teacher is one who instills the will to learn in others by role-modeling enthusiasm for learning. A teacher's excitement for her task imparts the desire to learn.

When performed effectively, teaching will prepare students to amplify what is taught and exceed the knowledge realm of the teacher. Teachers must focus on making wise choices in order to achieve noble outcomes. They have power to steer learners to understand not only what to *do*, but also what to *be*. Teachers stimulate effective listening skills. Being a good listener is the trademark of a great teacher.

Nathan M. Pusey suggested in *Daily Thoughts for School Administrators* that "the teacher's task is not to implant facts but to place the subject to be learned in front of the learner and through sympathy, emotion, imagination, and patience to awaken in the learner the restless drive for answers and insights which enlarge the personal life and give it meaning."[19]

A quotation of Galileo that has been passed down through the ages still holds true: "You cannot teach a man anything; you can only help him find it within himself."[20] To teach, then, is to stimulate another person to learn. Albert Einstein also affirmed that it is the supreme art of the teacher to awaken joy in creative expression in students. Karl Menninger summarizes the role of the teacher in these words: "What the teacher is, is more important than what he teaches."[21] A provocative thought is shared by Horace Mann in these words: "The essential requisites in a teacher's character are a love for children and a love for his work."[22] John Lubbock in *Daily Thoughts for School Administrators* provides this food for thought: "The important thing is not so much that every child should be taught, as that every child should be given the wish to learn."[23]

John Dewey clarified the importance of the active learning process by declaring that "we learn to do by doing."[24] In essence, to teach and learn must be closely related for achievement of excellence.

Joseph Epstein's 1981 publication *Masters: Portraits of Great Teachers* declares: "What all great teachers appear to have in common is love of their subject, an obvious satisfaction in ability to convince them that what they are being taught is deadly serious."[25]

Locke E. Bowman's 1980 publication *Teaching Today* affirmed that learners teach themselves and that it may be concluded, "learning is teaching—and teaching is learning."[26]

Growing Up Learning by Walter B. Barbe states that, "true learning is the ability to apply a skill or fact to real life."[27] He advises parents to assume the role of identifying children's strengths in order to build confidence. This role insures success while making learning fun. He suggests six ways that parents can be effective teachers:

1. Be aware how your child learns best—kinesthetically, visually, and editorially.
2. Be aware of how you learn best.
3. Provide your child with opportunities for success in his modality.
4. Discipline and reward your child according to how she learns best.
5. Always teach to your child's strengths rather than his weakness.
6. Help your child apply basic modality strategies to master more complex skills and concepts.

Teaching and learning are important in the process of peace making. In *Early Violence Prevention: Tools for Teachers of Young Children*, Ronald G. Slaby and others share evidence that the positive partnering of parents and teachers can prevent violence. Together, the teaching and learning team can empower positive relationships using healthy problem-solving activities.

Nationally validated programs, such as Head Start and Follow Through, have demonstrated that the key to success is the involvement of the home, school, and community. Home learning activities complement the classroom instructional components. Here is an example of a home learning project that can enhance the quality of character education.

HOME LEARNING ACTIVITY

TEACH AND LEARN BY CONCEIVING, BELIEVING, AND ACHIEVING

Answering these questions will guide you in your teaching and learning process:

- What is the topic?
- Why is it important?
- How is it used?
- What additional information will enhance character education?

Begin with a familiar topic such as a food or household article that all family members can use in a basic skill-building activity.

_____
_____
_____
_____

An initial topic for family teaching and learning could be apples. Family discussions will include the importance of eating this fruit to help promote healthy bodies.

- Read stories for discussion such as "Johnny Appleseed."
- Visit libraries and make appointments with media specialists to see and hear demonstrations on the importance of including apples in one's diet.
- Learn the history of apples: where and how they grow in various places.
- Study pictures of varieties of apples such as "Delicious," "McIntosh," "Jonathan," "Rome," "Stayman," and "Winesap."
- Visit a grocery store or fruit market to purchase at least one of each variety of apples. Compare the difference in taste, color, cost, size, seeds, etc.
- Slice and dice fractional parts of apples and compare the parts to the whole.
- Cut apples in half to discover stars in the center of each half.
- Plant apple seeds and observe growth of a plant.
- Eat in a variety of ways such as raw, in salads, applesauce, apple butter, apple-juice, or apple pie.
- Visit an apple orchard or someone with an apple tree to observe size and shape of the leaves, bark on the trees, and other discoveries. Interview apple growers to obtain answers to your family's questions.
- Write thank-you notes to all persons who shared information related to the study of apples.
- Make a journal of stories with illustrations of what you learned from this project and share it with others.

- Practice good manners, demonstrate respect, behave appropriately, and discuss ways in which acts of kindness can be shown to others during teaching and learning.
- Increase cooperation and collaboration among members of the family by communicating what has been learned from the project.
- As a family, create stories, poems, songs, finger plays, or quizzes related to your study of apples.
- Share how acts of kindness from others increased knowledge, skills, and creativity in the teaching and learning process.
- Discuss how asking questions about things you did not know increased knowledge and made additional fun for the family.
- Make group decisions about the next family teaching and learning project.

Chapter Eight

ENERGIZE SELF AND EXERCISE SUPPORT OF OTHERS

Have you ever seen a person who seemed to be upbeat, energized, and full of fun all the time? Have you ever been around a person who was so funny that you actually started laughing when you saw them? Well, all of us have good days and bad days. Some handle the bad days in an upbeat manner, believing that "tomorrow is another day, and it's got to be better than today." What a wonderful belief to embrace. Many of us may be able to *say* this, but not all of us are able to live it.

On the other hand, have you been around a person who never had anything good to say about anything? They just seemed to criticize everything and everybody. It was so bad that they were able to sufficiently depress everyone around them. This is an excellent way to de-energize and sap the support from everyone around this person. It is bad enough to depress yourself, but it is even worse to force that depression on others around you.

Family members must support each other. Coming home to loving and caring family members may be the only support and relief one receives within the course of a day, whether you are a child or an adult. Encouragement, respect, positive words, kindness, and hope may rest only within your home. Many of these character traits are the driving force behind a person's success. One should be able to take the love and support of family members and move beyond the difficulties of daily life. If we are serious about energizing self and exercising support of others, we must examine our personal families and improve upon our relationships with each other. The purpose of this chapter is to assist you in analyzing the strengths of the support system in your home. It is important to observe and be honest with your findings. Honesty is an extremely important character trait in holding a family firmly together.

It is appropriate for you to look at yourself and determine what role you play in keeping the family healthy, safe, and happy. It is also appropriate to honestly address what atmosphere you exude in your family circle. Oftentimes, we know the correct responses to these reflective questions. We know the right answers, but we are sometimes unaware of how our actions affect others.

Again, one of the most effective ways to jump-start a strong family character homemade program is to be completely honest with ourselves. This is not always pleasant. But, if we really want to create a better home for all family members, we must start first by looking within. Dr. Helen LeGette emphasizes the importance of honesty in *Parents, Kids and Character: 21 Strategies to Help Your Child Develop Good Character*. "Refuse to cover for your children or make excuses for their inappropriate behavior. Shielding children and youth from the logical consequences of their actions fails to teach them personal responsibility. It also undermines social customs and laws by giving them the impression that they are somehow exempt from the regulations that govern other's behavior."[28] Wonderful thought. If we shield our children at home and protect them from these consequences of the real world, how adequately are we preparing them when they go to school, out into the community, and out in the world? Are we helping them or harming them?

Standing firm and being honest also should provide consistency for everyone in the family. We must also be honest with adults in our daily dealing. Showing respect to others, honesty, caring, good manners, and trustworthiness are traits which should be a part of each family member's interactions.

We began this chapter by asking a series of questions for your reflection. Perhaps one of the most effective and genuine energizers is humor. There are many who are extremely skilled in making others laugh. It seems as though everything they say and do is funny. Sometimes, there are those who do not have to do anything, yet they are very humorous.

On the other hand, there are those of us who have to really work hard at making others laugh. Humor is a wonderful energizer and has its rightful place in the home. Humor has a way of energizing one as well as those around them. Laughter is a way of bonding together and showing support for others.

Reflect upon a family activity that ended with laughter. Did you, along with members of your family feel closer to each other? Did you feel more connected, at ease, and a part of a nurturing and supportive environment? Humor has a tendency to break down barriers and helps one to feel more at ease by allowing more open communication. Whenever open communication is present, there is the possibility of hope, encouragement, and support.

Think of an activity that may not necessarily be at the top of your list of favorite things to do. What about a physical examination? Getting an exam is a must, but it can be uncomfortable, somewhat embarrassing, and tends to make one a little nervous. If you can just hold on to a bit of humor and focus on that, the examination can move at a more peaceful and comfortable rate. Humor has a way of releasing tension, creating better results in many cases, and also helps us relax and boosts our attitudes.

The same can apply to our home environment. A smile and a bit of laughter can make a house a home centered around care, respect, and support. If you can establish a positive attitude, that can become contagious and be passed on to other family members. There are times when humor and support may be scarce and even non-existent. Think of those family times when there tends to be lots of tension, sharpness, and perhaps even resentment. Each household is different, so think of the specific circumstances in your home. As you develop your character education program, you should address those times and home situations which present high levels of stress, tension, and turmoil. One of the most effective ways of pinpointing a major family concern is to get the family together and talk about it! Different family members may have different ideas about what the problems are. That is one reason why it is important to hear from other family members. But keep in mind, as expressed by Dr. LeGette, "Remember that you are the adult!"[29]

The following activity will energize you and your family. It should also spark meaningful conversation, establish an atmosphere for airing family concerns, and also present possible solutions. It is important to provide two-way communication, respect for each other, honesty, creativity in problem-solving, and family support.

These questions are designed to get you talking with each other, raise the energy level, and attempt to pinpoint solutions in support of the family unit. In his book, *Five Needs Your Child **Must** Have Met at Home*, Ron Hutchcraft discusses the need for parents to support and encourage their children. "Cheerleaders. That's what parents are supposed to be for their kids. . . . But every parent can be a cheerleader in the sense of being your child's Chief Encourager, cheering for those strengths a child may minimize or miss."[30]

HOME LEARNING ACTIVITY

IDENTIFY FAMILY STRESS

Record your findings on this sheet:

1. Discuss the most stressful time of day for the family.

___

2. What makes this time of day so stressful?

___

3. Discuss how each family member can contribute to reducing the stress level.

___

4. Come to a consensus on specific ways you can each work to reduce stress.

___

5. Give this particular project two weeks, then reconvene to discuss the outcome. Record your successes here.

___

IDENTIFY TIMES OF RELAXATION

Record your findings on this sheet:

1. Discuss the most relaxing time of day with your family.

_____
_____
_____
_____
_____

2. What makes this time-of-the-day so relaxing?

_____
_____
_____
_____
_____

3. Discuss how family members can continue to ensure that this time remains peaceful.

_____
_____
_____
_____
_____

4. What is the primary difference in the two settings—peaceful vs. stressful?

_____
_____
_____
_____

5. How can the family transfer the relaxing attributes to impact the stressful parts of the day?

_____
_____
_____
_____

PARENT ACTIVITY

Talk with each other. Consider planning at least a thirty-minute celebration for your child or children. Look at each child and celebrate a strength or an area of improvement for each. Dress the role. Have the kids make some homemade pom-poms and celebration hats. This way, everyone is involved in this activity. You may also wish to videotape your family activity and review it in the future. Create a celebration "rap" and sing it or better still, rap it! The children will just love this. You say you can't do it. Well, try it. It will be fun, energizing for everyone, and expressing family support. Finish the activity with some good ole ice cream. Enjoy yourself and your family!

The cheerleader concept is a wonderful approach to energizing self and exercising support of others. Just as parents must serve as energizers for their children, children should also do likewise. So, go on—energize yourself and support your family.

CELEBRATION PLAN

Record your plan for a thirty-minute celebration of your child's strengths here.

_____
_____
_____
_____
_____
_____
_____
_____
_____
_____
_____
_____
_____
_____
_____
_____
_____
_____
_____
_____
_____

Reward Success

Chapter Nine

Chapter eight concluded by emphasizing the importance of serving as a cheerleader for your children. This holds true also for children serving as cheerleaders for parents. Each of us enjoys receiving a thank you, hearing the words *good job*, or any gesture of appreciation. Warm fuzzies encourage the spirit, mind, emotions, and the heart. These positive acknowledgments make one want to work a little bit harder. Isn't it amazing how small gestures can mean so much to the receiver?

We must now reflect on to what degree success should be acknowledged and rewarded. Do you reward successes only when designated goals are reached? Or, do you reward small steps of progress along the way? These are questions you should consider as you reward the successes of your family members. Rewarding successes internalizes the achievement of character traits including perseverance, honesty, sincerity, flexibility, and determination.

Progress toward any goal should be viewed as achievement. It is a good idea to celebrate the slightest movement in the right direction. Celebration could be something as simple as telling someone that they have done a good job or that they are improving. In most cases, this offers encouragement to continue moving toward the desired goal. This is one reason why cheerleading and coaching are so important in helping people achieve success.

It is equally as important for each of us to have an internal drive—feeling good about our level of success inch-by-inch. Letting children know that success is measured by small increments is vital. Even though movement may be slow and minute, that's okay. We must continue to instill in children that a feeling of inward pride may be the only reward that one may receive. The question still remains, do we reward everything?

In her book *What Do We Say? What Do We Do?*, Dr. Dorothy Rich warns of the dangers of over rewarding. "Rewards build motivation when they build children's appetites to develop . . . and when this development is strong enough to continue even though the rewards are withdrawn. Rewards can destroy motivation when they become the only reason that children work hard at home or do well in school. The danger is that when the reward stops, the child's motivation stops. That's when the reward does not fit the behavior we hope to teach."[31]

This is precisely what we were saying when we asked the question, do we reward everything and to what degree do we reward? You are now aware of the negative side of rewarding success. One of the major keys is to teach children the value of self-fulfillment even if no one else acknowledges the achievement. As parents and as educators, we frequently ask children to perform certain tasks. Unfortunately, we have also heard children ask, "What do I get if I am successful?" This is a signal that we should redefine our reward system.

As we move down the road toward rewarding success, character education becomes extremely valuable and very needed. What happens when one puts forth a tremendous effort and does not meet expectations? Has this ever happened to you as an adult? If so, how did you manage the feeling of failure while knowing beyond a shadow-of-doubt that you put forth every possible effort? In cases such as these, what happens to the level of confidence, perseverance, and motivation? It becomes our responsibility as adults to instill in children the will to keep on going even though they have failed at their attempt.

Children need to know that this is an issue with adults as well. We work from day-to-day and from year-to-year striving for a promotion. The promotion may or may not come, but we have the reassurance that we gave it our best. Self-fulfillment, pride, and motivation are deeply imbedded in our hearts. Mike Riera, family and adolescent counselor, discussed several family matters on the *Saturday Early Show* on June 30, 2001. Mr. Riera expressed the need for a family to sit down together and develop a mission statement. He emphasized the importance of discussing values during this time. If a mission statement is developed early on, the subject of rewarding success can be quickly brought to the table so everyone will know how the family will reward achievement. Now, let us move toward developing some fun family activities for rewarding success.

The "brag bulletin board" is a simple character-building activity that empowers each family member to become motivated, proud, and to seek inward fulfillment. This in itself is perhaps the greatest reward of success of all—feeling good about what you have accomplished even if no one else notices. This activity is designed to move you from the book to tangible meaningful activities in which all family members can engage. It also is a tool to help family members develop projects and activities which are useful and applicable to your entire family. We have not been successful if we cannot move you from mere words to application in your family.

Continue to look for other activities to enhance your brag board. Other family members may have suggestions. Remember, continue to work together and encourage each other on a daily basis. Those few words of encouragement that you offer your children during the early morning may be the only encouragement they receive during the entire day.

Character-building should move families to a higher level of caring and respect for themselves as well as for each other. If grounded firmly, these traits will go with each person from the home, to the school or job, and out in the community. You may feel like character development only happens within your home. But what if other families do likewise? Would this not make the world a better place? Would this not make living together a much easier task? Would this not make understanding and getting along with each other much better? It is our hope that these character-building activities will be a part of the lifestyle of many families.

HOME LEARNING ACTIVITY

REWARDING SUCCESS

- Establish a location in your home, preferably a high traffic area, and set up a brag bulletin board. Allow each family member to post several of their weekly accomplishments on Fridays. If there are younger children who cannot write, help them with this activity.
- Take the accomplishments lists down each week and assign a family member to save them in a "look what I've done" box or scrapbook. Review and read periodically at family meetings. Family Sunday dinnertime would also be an ideal time to discuss. You can even have separate brag day mealtime to discuss family member accomplishments. Go on and make this a b-i-g deal with your family!
- Another extension of this activity could be a once-a-month family celebration recapping the family's successful activities during that month. Further activities are left to the discretion of your family. Weave in a delightful discussion about various character education traits. Go on, celebrate with each other!

EXAMPLE FOR BRAG BOARD:

Guess what guys? I've lost three pounds!

Love you,
Mom 6/26/01

List some ideas of accomplishments you might share on your family's bulletin board.

_____
_____
_____
_____
_____
_____
_____
_____
_____
_____
_____
_____
_____
_____
_____
_____

Chapter Ten

ENGAGE IN TWO-WAY CONVERSATION

Positive two-way conversation enhances excellence in teaching and learning. It can create and recreate wholesome character that will find needs and fill them for peace on earth and goodwill toward all mankind.

An Irish proverb says "a cure for all sorrows is conversation." Likewise, conversation can serve as a booster through peaceful communication which enhances the growth and development of mind and soul.

Many years ago an interesting advertisement was circulated by American Telephone and Telegraph that said: "At least talk to each other. To communicate is the beginning of understanding." Ralph Waldo Emerson underscored this statement with these words: "Conversation is the laboratory of the student."

Donald Walton's book *Are You Communicating? You Can't Manage Without It*, shares numerous ideas for improving communication. Walton explains that conversation is the kind of interchange between people that falls into three categories: social, emotional, and intellectual. For example:

- *Emotional Conversation*
  Intensely personal—sharing of intimate feelings.
- *Social Conversation*
  Meaningless phrases and clichés—small talk that builds relationships.
- *Intellectual Conversation*
  Conveys information and ideas—can also be persuasive.[32]

In the publication *Smart Speaking: Sixty Second Strategies* by Schloff and Yudkin, the authors explain that there are certain key beliefs and attitudes one can find in conversations of outgoing people. They let their conversations extend beyond their inner circles and find easy openers based on people's interests.

In Harvey Mackay's publication *Dig Your Well Before You Are Thirsty*, he emphasizes the importance of networking in the process of communication. He illustrates in a top-ten list the most important things a network can do. Among them are maxims that explain how the weakness of an individual can be strengthened by a group and that a caring and concerned group can serve as a magic mirror for self-improvement.

In a speech emphasizing the importance of communication between the school and the community, Mamchak and Mamchak share this message:

> When we communicate, we share our feelings, and there is an exchange of information that can open the minds of both sides. Through the process of communication can come understanding, and with understanding

comes a new commitment. A commitment to further communication; a commitment for finding out for ourselves the exact nature of the problem; a commitment to work together, the school and the home—two of the most powerful forces on earth—to seek for remedies; to seek for solutions; to seek for the common ground that will eventually allow our schools and our children to be the best they are capable of becoming.[33]

The real art of conversation as confirmed by Braude, compiler and editor of *Handbook of Stories for Toastmasters and Speakers,* is not only to say the right thing, but to not say the wrong thing at the tempting moment.

Quinn's *365 Meditations for Teachers* emphasized that "effective communication uses a common language spoken at a common level." He further states that "communication is the river and understanding is the ocean—Every river leads to the ocean."[34] Two-way conversation results in positive messages of faith, hope, and unconditional love for self and others.

In *The Living Classroom,* David Armington asserts that learning and moral development are communicated through an overall moral climate rather than specific lessons. The positive atmosphere itself is educative. According to Maggart and Zintz, "The significant adult in the child's environment expands the child's language competence just by talking and thereby providing a model."[35]

A stimulating suggestion was offered by William Lampton in his publication *The Complete Communicator*. He stated, "Asking for advice ranks among our highest communication privileges. Calling on the collective wisdom of achievers, we're almost sure to surpass our own solitary judgment."[36]

In the book, *Living, Loving and Learning,* Leo Buscaglia shared the importance of risk-taking in learning to trust and believe. He stated, "Then I think we need to teach children the importance of others, and that they cannot grow in this world without taking in others. The more worlds they take in, these unique worlds, the more they can become."[37]

Two-way conversation between parents and children can be a driving force for success in home, school, and community activities. Support systems outside of the home can reinforce the character-building work you are doing in your home. A network of communicators in the community benefit present and future generations by being positive role models. The following list offers ideas to help you enhance two-way conversation in your family:

- Engage in two-way conversation with family members to discuss the responsibility of each person for making family life healthy, happy, and terrific.
- Visit the library and choose books that are developmentally appropriate for each age group and that are interesting to each reader. Discuss them with each other. (Preschoolers can choose picture books.)
- Discuss definitions of these words: respect, responsibility, behavior, character, and values.
- Set weekly goals to be accomplished by each family member. For example:

1. Learn a poem.
2. Do homework everyday at a specified time.
3. Keep a journal. Write or draw in it each day.
4. Learn the definition of a new word each day.
5. Turn off the television and engage in two-way conversation for a specific period daily.
6. Go to the library at least once a week.
7. Go on a short trip as a family to the grocery store, museum, or some other place of interest. Discuss what you observed.

List some of your own ideas for activities that could improve your family's two-way conversation.
_____
_____

HOME LEARNING ACTIVITY

Read and discuss the enclosed parent-child agreement that was shared by an unknown author.

A PARENT AND CHILD AGREEMENT

We have a very special relationship composed of two individuals,
    One who is a parent who once was a child,
    The other a child who may someday be a parent.

Each of us has a power and a choice:
    To hurt or to help; To be cruel or to be kind;
    To put down or support;
    To accuse or to trust the other.

We can talk to each other
    So that there is an open sharing of feelings, wants, needs, and ideas.

We can listen to each other
    So that hearing and understanding happen between us.

Each of us is an individual
    And must continue to protect the right.
    Yet, we can so live our lives,
    Make our decisions,
    And determine our needs—
    That the other will feel proud.

Let us agree to:
    Never expect or require too much of each other;
    Be willing to compromise when we are in conflict;
    Not attack, label, or insult each other;
    Avoid the unfavorable comparison with other parents and children;
    And to never be right at the expense of the other being wrong.

Let us mutually seek
    Peace and contentment, consideration and respect,
    friendship and love when we are together,
    If this says it, like it is for you—

We have an agreement between us

Let's sign!   _____ (parent)

                 _____ (child)

—Author unknown

Chapter Eleven

Deepen the Well of Security

Have you ever been in a potentially dangerous situation, but you felt safe and secure? Think about why you felt safe. More than likely, someone in your life provided an atmosphere of protection for you. Many of us can recall our childhood days and reflect back on many situations which posed a threat but because of something or someone, we felt secure in that no hurt, harm, or danger would come upon us. That something or someone in our lives helped to deepen the well of security. Today, whether we are parents or caretakers of children, we must assume this responsibility and help our children and families feel safe.

Home should be a safe haven for all of its occupants. Schools and communities should also be safe. Examine the environment that you and your family can control. Naturally, you love your home because you consider it to be secure and safe, but there is always room for improvement. How can you deepen the well of security in your present home environment? Deepening the well of security sharpens those character traits that are already present within your family structure.

Strengthening security within the home brings family members closer together. The caring and respect traits are practiced in the home. There is a high level of concern for the happiness and safety of others. The focus is not on self, but on others. "At the heart of good character is a sense of caring and concern for others. Numerous opportunities for family service projects exist in every community, and even young children can participate."[38]

Caring and concern are paramount when strengthening the security of the home. If these attributes are helpful in strengthening a community, look at what they can do for your entire family. There are many family activities that can help deepen the well of security.

Homemade character education programs are developed, shared, and revised by members of the household. Including everyone helps to provide a high level of security among family members. Quite often young people are ashamed to share their fears with adults and family members. It is our responsibility as adults to break down these walls and open the door to honest and up-front communication. Many do not want to be perceived as fearful. However, they are afraid, nervous, or uncomfortable. As adults, we must let them know that everyone is afraid of something at some time in their lives. But with support, caring, and concern, we can certainly deepen the well of security.

Deepening the well does not say that all of our fears and uncertainties vanish, but it simply lets us know that if we do fear or if we are nervous, there is someone who will stand by and support us. Talking about our insecurities will pave the way for family members to offer an arm of support. Children as well as adults need to express their fears. We can learn so much from each other. Just because we are adults does not mean that we have all the answers. Many times, young people say things that allow us to reevaluate our thoughts and the direction in which we are moving. We are adults, and we have been fortunate to experience many situations that our children have not yet experienced. But our children still have something wonderful to offer us.

A Nick Jr. production of *Little Bill* clearly depicted the traits of family caring, sharing, and concern on a Saturday series titled "The Promise." The Saturday morning cartoon showed how Little Bill wanted to take something to school which was different and share it with his classmates. He was given a very special trophy won earlier by his sister. It was special to her. Well, he took it and shared, but he also managed to break it. It was only through telling the truth and giving back something that was special to him that he learned to feel more secure.

Deepening the well of security is perhaps one of the most important elements for family happiness and success. It again involves everyone working together to ensure the safety of each member dwelling within the walls of the home. One family member may be able to contribute to the security in the home in one manner while another can contribute in another way. The important thing is that all are aware and do what they can to make the home a safe and happy haven.

It is important to look at a family activity which will enable you to analyze the level of security within your home. The family needs to gather together to perform the deepening the well of security activity. With this activity in place, the entire family will be able to construct a picture of those things which feel threatening, unsafe, and cold as opposed to those which empower family members to feel safe, happy, maintain a high level of motivation, self-esteem, honesty, care, and concern for everyone. Map out the concerns and move forward to embrace success.

Once you have outlined and discussed the insecurities, go back and discuss how they can be eliminated from the list.

An insecurity could be something like failing to call home and letting other family members know that you will be late coming home or late for dinner. Addressing this may be something as simple as picking up a telephone and calling home and letting the family know that you are all right and will be late.

Quite often, we do not even know when we have failed to be polite and cognizant of the concerns and feelings of others. Many times, people do things that have a negative effect on others without even realizing it. Also, many times we fail to do things not knowing that it creates insecurity among family members. Pinpointing and addressing insecurities is a move towards politeness, which is truly an outstanding character trait. It would also be a very strong family activity to set aside a "politeness week" in your home. How do you think the week would progress if every family member signed a pledge to be polite and courteous for one week?

Set aside special family time to share the activity that you completed earlier. Some family members may be shocked to see what disturbs or upsets other family members. As a part of your conversation, you may hear, "I didn't know that!" Many activities suggested in this manual insist on family conversation and exchange of thoughts and ideas. So much can be shared and learned through talking with each other. The well of security can be deepened by talking with, listening to, and sharing with each other.

As a part of your homemade character education program you have been given an opportunity to discuss and post areas of insecurities. Of equal importance is to know what makes family members feel secure within the home. The next activity is a way of discussing and pinpointing those attributes which make you feel happy and secure. Again, you may hear, "I didn't know that!" This will give you tangible documentation, and family chat time can provide valuable dialogue and input. Activities such as these will enhance your homemade character education program.

After the next activity, concentrate on the valuable and productive outcomes. Challenge each other to strive to make the home a safer and warmer haven. These activities are geared to help you develop a stronger sense of communicating honestly, instilling family pride, caring, sharing, responsibility, and respect for each other's feelings. Go ahead and express those things which make you feel secure and safe.

Home Learning Activity

Deepening the Well of Security

What is the insecurity?	What can I do?	Who will benefit?

Deepening the Well of Security

What makes me feel secure?	Who is responsible for this security?	Who benefits?

Chapter Twelve

UNDERSTAND RULES FOR ACCEPTABLE BEHAVIOR

 The adage "more learning is caught than taught" is a guideline for how concepts are internalized in the teaching and learning process. In order to understand rules of appropriate behavior, role models need to demonstrate what is acceptable in our society.

In an *Early Childhood Practicum Guide* for student teachers, Machado and Meyer (1984) based their advice on Maslow's hierarchy of needs and on Erikson's theory of psychosocial development.

Machado and Meyer did further research and shared their findings about behavior origins. They concluded that:

1. All behavior is meaningful to the child, even that which an adult might call negative.
2. All behavior is reinforced by the environment (people, places, and things).[39]

Faced with numerous reports of aggressive behavior by children, Slaby and other researchers wrote *Early Violence Prevention: Tools for Teachers of Young Children*. The National Association for the Education of Young Children (NAEYC) circulated it to provide tools for modifying undesirable behavior. The researchers reported that unacceptable patterns of behavior resulted from several contributing causes. Among them are "experiencing victimization, being encouraged and rewarded for behaving aggressively, witnessing powerful violent models or watching portrayals of violence on television."[40] These suggestions were among several offered by Slaby and associates to help children with aggressive behavior patterns:

- Design individualized behavior-change plans to help children who behave aggressively.
- Help children focus on self-control.
- Promote extra support to children. Let them know that their feelings and needs are important and you care about them, and that you can help them to make changes in their habits.

In 2001, the Leadership Conference in Minnesota was sponsored by Pi Lambda Theta, an International Honor Society in Education. Four presenters from Frederick County, Maryland, conducted an impressive workshop on "Character Counts When Dealing With Tolerance." They shared fantastic ideas for promoting multicultural tolerance through character counts education.

They shared three core beliefs for developing character when it counts:

43

1. There are enduring universal beliefs that distinguish right from wrong and define good character.
2. Who you are makes the difference in all relationships.
3. Character is not hereditary. It must be developed by example and demand.

The team explained these six pillars of character:

- Trustworthiness
- Respect
- Responsibility
- Fairness
- Caring
- Citizenship

The discussion convinced all participants that through concerted efforts of home, school, and community, children can learn and understand rules of acceptable behavior.

The Philadelphia Child Guidance Center with Jack McGuire published *Your Child's Emotional Health*. They stated: *"Behavior Modeling* is a therapeutic technique by means of which a child is taught or encouraged to replace negative behaviors with more positive ones. The teaching or encouraging process involves modifying the way each parent or caretaker interacts with the child so that he/she learns to behave more constructively."[41]

Linda and Richard Eyre shared *Steps to a Strong Family* in 1994. They offered three conceptually simple steps for ensuring a strong family:

1. Rules or laws (a legal system);
2. A way of allocating resources (an economy);
3. Strong traditions based on shared values. (p. 13)

According to these authors, these three steps will result in "a strong family to work on, sort out, to communicate and implement together."[42]

Discussing how diversity among family members can be utilized to overcome obstacles in daily life, Denise Lang's book *Family Harmony: Coping With Your Challenging Relatives* presented five bridge-building supports for family harmony:

1. Building communication skills among family members.
2. Dump that "supposed to's" and adjust your expectation level.
3. Tolerance versus endorsement. Learning that tolerance of another's actions does not necessarily mean we gladly endorse the choice. It lays the foundation for good communication building and a productive relationship.
4. Humor warp—use humor to laugh at the various rituals of family members rather than tensing up.
5. Adoption of a surrogate family when family members do not support ones needs. Avoid combative activities and find an outside support system.[43]

Several of these authors addressed the need to work with young children to prevent unacceptable behavior and to cultivate acceptable behavior. Myrna Schure developed a program for preteens called "I Can Problem Solve" for eight to twelve year olds. She outlined five skills needed to become good problem solvers:

1. Understanding another's feelings and point of view
2. Understanding motives
3. Finding alternative solutions
4. Considering consequences
5. Sequenced planning[44]

According to Schure, "All children, no matter how skilled they are, will face new and unexpected challenges as they grow, and their parents won't always be there to protect them. Parents who let their children know that they value *thinking* about what to do and say will raise children who will be more likely to use the "I Can Problem Solve (ICPS) skills when they need them."[45]

Ideas for working effectively with adolescents were given by Jeanette Shalov and others in a publication, *You Can Say No to Your Teenager and Other Strategies for Effective Parenting in the 1990s*. She reminded readers that "An adolescent is a child . . . is in the process of growing into an adult. However, the growth process involves a myriad of annoying, perplexing and frightening behavior patterns, including (but unfortunately not limited to) lack of impulse control, the need for instant gratification, identity confusion, a desire for separation and independence, challenge to authority." . . . She reminded parents that they are also growing into a new role: "part of that growth process [is that] you feel shock, disappointment, guilt, confusion, competition, resentment."[46]

Shalov clarifies that the dual role of parents and adolescents is a process of recognizing acceptable behavior and of determining which behaviors are normal and which are not and to channel them in a "creative purposeful direction."[47] She explains the difference in values and boundaries and indicates that adolescents should understand that boundaries are flexible but values are not. Parents are responsible for saying "no" to an adolescent when values are being violated.[48]

Clemes and Bean cowrote *Self-Esteem: The Key to Your Child's Well-Being*. They explained that in developing high, healthy self-esteemers, children should be trained to take responsibility to "adopt a pattern of appropriate behavior based on your requirements and by reaching realistic conclusions from every experience."[49] They also stated that, "The role of parents must be structured to give children support when they need it; show interest in what children do; and share chores as recognition of their efforts."[50]

In our perception, these guidelines will empower families to build character by understanding aceptable behavior.

A Act responsibly at all times.
C Commit to making wise choices.
C Care for self and others.
E Expect to succeed.
P Plan activities for goal setting.
T Think of ways to solve problems.
A Achieve excellence.
B Believe in yourself.
L Love unconditionally.
E Earn respect by being respectable.

B Be bridge-builders of support for self and others.
E Examine family values and develop support systems for implementing them.
H Help to solve problems in home, school, and community.
A Adjust activities to find needs and fill them.
V Values must be clarified to understand the rules of acceptable behavior.
I Imagine the results of cooperation of children, parents, and other caregivers in bringing peace and harmony in the home, school, and community.
O Organize a team of positive thinkers and doers in building bridges of support.
R Reward family units for teamwork in planning, implementing, and understanding rules for acceptable behavior.

HOME LEARNING ACTIVITY

ACCEPTABLE BEHAVIOR

Plan a family visit to the children's department of your local library. Ask the media specialist on duty to recommend several books on various age levels related to character education that will empower each family member to understand rules for acceptable behavior. Here are a few possibilites:

Easy Picture Books
- Hoban, Russell. *Best Friends for Frances.* New York: Harper Collins Publishers, 1969.
- Hoffman, Mary. *Amazing Grace.* New York: Dial Books for Young Readers, 1991.
- Johnston, Tony. *Grandpa's Song.* New York: Dial Books for Young Readers, 1991.
- Joose, Barbara M. *Mama Do You Love Me?* San Francisco, Calif.: Chronicle Books, 1991.
- Krauss, Ruth. *You're Just What I Need.* New York: Harper-Collins, 1998.
- Lester, Helen. *It Wasn't My Fault.* New York: Houghton Mifflin Co., 1985.

Junior and Adult Books
- Bernstein, Joanne and Masha Kabakow Rudman. *Books To Help Children Cope With Separation and Loss: An Annotated Bibliography,* Volume 3. New York: R. R. Rowker, 1989.
- Gockley, Gil and Tanya Tihansky. *Loving Is Natural, Parenting Is Not: Creating a Value Centered Family.* New York: Coleman Press, 1997.
- Lewis, Steven. *The ABCs of Real Family Values.* New York: Penguin Putnam, 1998.
- Nelson, Jane et. al. *Positive Discipline: Laying Foundation for Raising a Capable Confident Child.* Rocklin, Calif.: Prima Publishers, 1998.
- Richards, Norma. *Dreamers and Doers: Inventors Who Changed Our World.* New York: Atheneum, 1984.

All family members, from preschoolers to adults, will select their favorite books. Have a family discussion on the favorite parts of each book. Answer the following questions:

1. What is your definition of behavior?

_____
_____

2. Why is it important to understand rules of acceptable behavior?

_____
_____

Understand Rules for Acceptable Behavior 47

3. List some acceptable rules that are used in your family.

_____
_____
_____
_____
_____

4. Share some ways that will help you improve your behavior.

_____
_____
_____
_____
_____

Make a family booklet with illustrations and stories about family goals, values, and acceptable behaviors in home, school, the workplace, and community.

Chapter Thirteen

COMMUNICATE ON A TWO-WAY BASIS

Put yourself in this situation: You are experiencing severe pain with your left elbow. You make an appointment to visit your doctor to get an examination along with some relief. On your visit, you are not allowed to speak with your doctor but to only say to her, "Fix me." You cannot say anything other than that, nor can you use any type of physical gestures or sounds to indicate the location or intensity of your pain and discomfort. When the doctor asks you questions about your complaint, you can only look at her. Your doctor's communication to you is well-established and thoroughly in order during this visit. How much can be accomplished during your visit? Do you feel that you will get some relief? If so, how long will it take before you will get relief from pain?

As this example shows, one-sided communication can result in delay, added problems, misunderstanding, confusion, pain and suffering, and a feeling of total failure. Opening the door to two-way communication is vital in a homemade character education program. You can probably think of other situations where the end results could be devastating if communication only existed from one side.

What does two-way communication foster in a home? As you read this chapter, think of ways your family can open the door of communication and give everybody the opportunity to express themselves.

Adults as well as children should feel close enough to talk with each other. One of the joys of communicating is the ability to hear others and respect their opinions. Communication sets the stage for the possibility of changing situations. If you had been able to talk with your doctor, you could have perhaps eliminated extra testing, cut back on time, and lessened the confusion on both sides.

As we refer back to *Parents, Kids and Character: 21 Strategies to Help Your Children Develop Good Character,* we see strategies which stress *togetherness*, *with*, and *involved*. Each word implies that two-way communication among family members is imminent. The strategies indicate that getting family members together encourages sharing, discussing, and exchanging. Strategy five instructs us to, "Have family meals together without television as often as possible. Mealtime is an excellent time for parents to talk with and listen to their children and to strengthen family ties."[51] Again, perhaps three of the most powerful binding words in this strategy are "with" and "listen to." These terms automatically imply communication moving back and forth between people. The conversation is not dictated by parents or the children, but both share equally. Family members are both talking with and listening to each other. These actions produce a healthy and well-respected homemade character education program.

What other time of the day is more productive in sharing and talking with each other than during a special meal? The meal does not have to be a long full-course meal, but just sitting down for a few minutes and sharing together improves communication among family members. It is almost like there is something magical about eating a meal together. Food somehow soothes the body, satisfies the appetite, and invokes laughter. One conversation leads to another. This time of the day with family members brings about a certain level of comfort and calmness.

The family will have many other opportunities to come together and share. How are others to know how you feel or what upsets you if you do not tell them and communicate with them?

Many doors have been closed, many opportunities for progress have been lost, even friendships have suffered simply because people have not honestly shared their feelings. There is always a right way and a wrong way to express feelings and beliefs. As we share our feelings, we also must *respect* the feelings of others.

Let us look at a simple example. Mom may know that she is extremely talented when it comes to cooking potato pie. But you may not like potato pie! This by no means is a negative reflection of mom's ability to cook this dessert. She may even be a master at cooking this particular food. However, that does not increase your appetite for potato pie. Now your ability to effectively communicate with her will be tested. There is a way to approach her and make her aware of your dislike for this food. Think about when you could approach her, trying to find the best time and the most conducive atmosphere in which to break the news. If you think through the process, more than likely you can develop an atmosphere where open discussion will take place and also you may be able to discuss alternatives to this problem. There is a chance that she will appreciate you telling her the truth, and she also will be able to share her feelings and ideas with you.

Will two-way communication always end on a positive note? Of course not. But one thing you can control is being honest and up-front with your family, making sure that you have not misled them. Mom may be a little hurt at first, but more than likely she will offer to make a super banana pudding!

Two-way communication can certainly open the door to a higher level of:

- Honesty
- Caring
- Trustworthiness
- Respectfulness
- Compassion
- Consideration for the feelings of all family members

Dr. James Shaw stresses in his book, *Jack and Jill, Why They Kill: A Parents Guide*, the importance of establishing two-way communication with your children. "Include your child in even sensitive problematic or otherwise important family situations. Ask your child how and what he feels. Children who have constant, positive communication with their parents have better self-esteem than children who do not."[52] Building these kinds of relationships with your children can affect them from childhood throughout adulthood. Just think how powerful establishing positive and two-way communication can be in the lives of your children. It is quite possible that if you do this with your children, they will in turn provide a nurturing environment with their children by establishing strong two-way communication and empowering them to feel good about themselves. This is a gift that can move from generation to generation. With all of this in mind, let us move to a wonderful family activity which will allow families to emphasize two-way communication.

HOME LEARNING ACTIVITY

PRACTICING TWO-WAY COMMUNICATION

Discuss with your family and agree upon a favorite holiday when family members can spend quality time together. After you decide, list activities you would like to do together and discuss why these activities are important.

_____
_____
_____
_____

This activity will spark lively discussion and may even bring to light activities you were not aware were important to other family members. These activities will establish some common ground between the youth, middle-aged, and older adults.

Save these suggestions and recommendations until the designated holiday. At that time, follow through as a family with the family activities. Have a great holiday together and have fun!

TWO-WAY COMMUNICATION GAME

Be creative as a family and design a verbal and/or silent charade family game.

Example: Verbal Game for the Yuletide Season
One family member is selected to be a holiday tree with a costume of several branches. Other family members make ornaments to decorate the tree. When each ornament is attached, the family member will describe it. For instance, "I made a blue angel to protect you;" another member may say "I made a yellow star to give you a bright light to shine like a good citizen," etc. When all ornaments are placed, the member serving as a tree will make an acceptance speech giving thanks for the gifts.

Example: Silent Charade
An artificial tree is made and each family member will dramatize the name of an ornament for the tree. For instance, a halo around the head with outstretched arms will represent an angel. Another will use hands and fingers to represent a star, etc.

Chapter Fourteen

ADMIT MISTAKES AND IMPROVE

 In our career as educators and as participants in home, school, and community activities, we have been faced with mistakes that caused us concerns. We have learned to make corrections and have experienced growth as we have overcome obstacles that impeded our progress.

Many sources of strength have empowered us to admit our mistakes, to apologize for our errors in judgment, and have helped us make wise choices in the art of communication. Reading self-help books and thinking before speaking are tools we have found useful in reducing the number of mistakes we have made. We have also learned that it is important to apologize for inappropriate reactions. Positive restructuring of our behavior promoted growth in our search for continuous improvement in daily living.

Quinn's book *365 Meditations for Teachers* has provided boundless food for thought. An example is found in his wisdom shared for December 26. He stated: "While difficult and awkward, the experience of admitting wrongdoing clears the forest of deceit, paves the road of character, and opens up the wilderness to progress."[53] Constant reading and discussion of this quotation enabled us to do more soul-searching to avoid making mistakes and to develop strength to apologize, ask for forgiveness, and improve our thoughts and actions.

Developing a 21st Century Mind by Marsha Sinetar offered advice we have found helpful:

> We can learn to apply the skill of using our flaws and limitations to a wider life canvas. In part, our ability to go with what we are comes with emotional maturity. Additionally, a mix of cognitive strengths provides the heightened awareness that lets us use our blemishes creatively. If we do this we advance, rather than defeat our life. For instance, when we are intellectually robust, we can examine ourselves honestly, perhaps with a touch of good humor. Eventually, we find a nest fit between what we do well and what we must let others do for us and our own best solution.[54]

It is our belief that reduction of mistakes will be made when we make conscious efforts to live by the Golden Rule of doing unto others what we would have them do unto us. In *The Ultimate Secrets of Self-Confidence,* Robert Anthony stated, "If you are to break out of the comfort zone you created, you must make friends with failure. When you decide to give up your need for approval, it won't matter how many mistakes you make as long as you reach your ultimate goal."[55]

During informal conversations with intergenerational diverse populations who, in our perception, are healthy high self-esteemers, we have asked several diverse persons with high self-esteem to react to the phrase, "Admit mistakes and improve." A summary of comments from some of the young children said: "When you make a mistake by doing or saying something wrong, if you apologize you won't be punished by having to take 'time-out' from playing." "If you admit you made a mistake your parents will continue to love you for telling the truth." Some older children stated, "If you apologize for making mistakes you will be forgiven." "Try not to make the same mistake twice and learn from doing wrong." Adults interviewed said: "Ask for forgiveness and pray that you will be guided to stop making mistakes." "Think before you speak or react and you will not make mistakes."

Jacob M. Braude has collected and edited several volumes of quotations on numerous topics. In his *Complete Speakers and Toastmasters Library,* he affirmed: "Mistakes are a great educator when one is earnest enough to admit them and willing to learn from them. . . . The man who never makes mistakes loses a great many chances to learn something. . . . A mistake at least proves somebody stopped talking long enough to do something."[56]

Braude also shared this idea: "A hundred mistakes is a liberal education if you learn something from each one." He quoted Mother Teresa of Calcutta as saying: "I would rather make mistakes in kindness and compassion than work miracles in unkindness and hardness." He stated that Confucius said: "A man who has made a mistake and doesn't correct it is making another mistake."[57]

In Braude's *Lifetime Speakers Encyclopedia Volume I* he reported that Wang Yang Ming said: "The sages do not consider that making no mistake is a blessing. They believe rather that the great virtue of man lies in his ability to correct his mistakes and continue to make a new man of himself."[58]

Braude's volume on quips, quotes, and anecdotes shared these "Six Mistakes of Man" as outlined by Cicero, the Roman philosopher and statesman:

1. The delusion that personal gain is made by crushing others.
2. The tendency to worry about things that cannot be changed.
3. Insisting that a thing is impossible because we cannot accomplish it.
4. Refusing to set aside trivial preferences.
5. Neglecting development and refinement of the mind and not acquiring the habit of reading and study.
6. Attempting to compel others to live as we do.[59]

We conclude that, as human beings, we will make mistakes. In order to overcome obstacles that impede our progress towards success, we must admit each error and develop guidelines for learning.

Healthy, happy, and terrific minds, bodies, and souls of all human beings will be evidenced when we make conscious efforts to admit mistakes. As we improve in developing caring, concerned, and committed attitudes, we will seek forgiveness and learn to share unconditional love.

HOME LEARNING ACTIVITY

ADMIT MISTAKES

Hold a family meeting for the purpose of sharing mistakes you all have made at home, school, the workplace, and in community activities.

List each family member's mistakes:

_____
_____
_____
_____

Discuss a lesson learned from admitting the mistake:

_____
_____
_____
_____

Discuss mistakes that people have made before making inventions that made our world a better place. Go to your local library and find books that will help you find answers. Examples: George Washington Carver, Madame C. J. Walker, Thomas A. Edison, and Benjamin Banneker.

Make a family booklet with stories and pictures of favorite achievers in history and current people who are successful in their careers because they learned from their mistakes.

Discuss career goals of each family member and share strategies for achieving in spite of mistakes they have made along the way.

Give sincere, honest praise to each family member for participating in this activity.

Chapter Fifteen

Think Before You Speak

 The words we speak to other human beings can rest in their hearts and minds for the rest of their lives. Think of that type of power. Words are powerful and can encourage as well as discourage. The timing of what we say and how we say it can truly change someone's life. The emotional impact could be different today than tomorrow. So many factors in our daily living can change our attitudes, outlooks, and the way we hear, comprehend, and process what is taking place around us. Words can change our lives; they can change our outlook on what is happening around us. Words can move our spirits to the top of the mountain or drop them down to the lowest level in the valley. How do we interpret what we hear?

This chapter is devoted to addressing how words impact our lives whether we are children or adults. Even as adults, we frequently wrestle with what is said to us and how it is said. We can look back on our lives and remember words expressed to us by significant adults and caretakers.

There were those adults who constantly repeated that we could do it, we could achieve, and we could make it. Many of us have been cheered, reassured, and praised as we graduated from the tricycle to the bicycle. Even though we may have fallen off, we were encouraged to get back on and try again, again, and again. We not only heard the spoken words, but the tone used also coerced us into getting up and trying again. The tone indicated that they believed that we could do it! Many of us have transferred these same words of encouragement to our children as they tried to ride their bikes or got their first haircuts. Before we expressed those words of encouragement, we often thought about the most exciting words to help to make the child's goal even more achievable. We were aware that *certain words*, expressed in a *certain manner* in a *particular tone* and at a *specific time*, could determine the success or failure of our children.

There were also other times when we were spoken to with sharp words which remain with us to this very day. We have said things to our loved ones that we have later regretted. We did not think before we spoke. We have also left things unsaid that should have been said. Words can build up and words can tear down. The study of this chapter reemphasizes being considerate, caring, and understanding as you mold and shape your family character education program.

We remain constant when it comes to criticizing others, but we become more sluggish when it comes to saying something positive about another person. It is much easier, more pleasant, and considerate to say positive things.

As we reflect back with our families on what we have accomplished thus far, we should see that each family member has contributed to the success of our family character program. Respecting the feelings of others is so very important in shaping and maintaining a harmonious home. Let us now put our skills and creativity to work for another family activity geared around thinking before we speak.

Knowing that positive words of truth are extremely important, realize that there are times when we must speak firmly, justly, and with authority. Others may take this as being cold, ruthless, and insensitive, but you are the parent. If directions and information need to be given, you must do so. Parents and significant adults have to take the leadership role and express what they mean and what they feel is the right thing to do.

Building strong character in the home requires that we express ourselves, but along with that to think before we speak. Expressing to others out of anger can be devastating. Keeping one's cool can be difficult at times, but it will gain respect. Expressing firmly what is expected and why will equally gain respect. This is not to say that all directions will be received with cheers and flips, but more than likely, children will respect them along with knowing that you as parents are the ones who are in charge.

You have observed that many of the family activities throughout this manual have been centered around family conversations. Getting together and talking honestly with each other is a key factor in learning about each other, respecting each other, and getting to the root of each individual's interests. What we say to each other and how we say it can certainly make a house a home. Cultivating character education traits in the home will bring family members closer together and more apt to discuss personal matters.

It is a must that we as adults take time to talk *with* children and not always just talk *to* them. If we fail to do so, they will find an alternative. It could be talking with a peer and even using the computer to talk with others who may not have the best interest of the child in mind.

More and more children are resorting to going to chat rooms. Why? Research shows that many youth who resort to violence, whether in the streets or in schools, express that family members were not there, or they did not take the time to talk with them and listen to what they were saying. "I don't have time" can be one of the most devastating statements an adult can say to a child. Words can tear apart, push away, and destroy. Think before you speak!

We spoke early on about *what we say* and *how we say it*. This is something that adults must be in tune with as they communicate with young people. How do you interpret "I don't have time?" How would a young person interpret the same statement? The interpretation of words may be different to different age groups. Along with that, how it is said and in what tone is left to individual interpretation. Think before you speak. Words can be extremely powerful.

HOME LEARNING ACTIVITY

THINKING BEFORE WE SPEAK

- Have family members record on a sticky note the positive comments that others in the household have expressed to them for one week.
- Set up a special location in the home where these positive comments can be posted. It should be a well-traveled area.
- Whenever someone says something that hurts you, go and read one of the positive comments.
- Respond to the one who made a hurtful comment. Let him/her know that words can hurt you.
- Meet together and discuss your feelings during the seven-day period.

WORDS CAN
Help you,
Hurt you,
Mold you
and
Console you

WORDS CAN
Sadden you,
Anger you,
Tease you,
and
Appease you

WORDS CAN
Humor you,
Motivate you,
Pacify you,
and
Satisfy you

WORDS CAN
Heal you,
Confuse you,
Destroy you,
and
Annoy you

WORDS CAN
Tear you apart,
Mend you back,
Bond you,
and
Alarm you

BE CAREFUL HOW YOU USE THEM, *THINK BEFORE YOU SPEAK*.

Think Before You Speak

Chapter Sixteen

Interact for Positive Outcomes

Teamwork is a must for empowering family members and others to interact in the learning process. When members of a family and other caretakers engage in finding needs and filling them, areas that need improvement are strengthened. Operating on the premise that the greatest room in the world is the room for improvement, interaction will be focused on building towers of positive reinforcement. Planning, implementing, and assessing the structure of goal setting and decision making is an essential part of this process.

A primary responsibility in the process of strengthening character education is the desire to form a bond of support for all participants. This bond will increase in a network of power when the roots of the trees of faith, hope, and unconditional love grow deeper and branches spread upward and outward to touch the lives of others. This growth is the result of connecting structured relationships and interacting in positive ways.

Mapping strategies for improvement will incorporate knowledge, skills, and creative approaches to increase the power of positive thinking in every area of life. Seven major areas of interaction are:

1. *Physical Strengths*—Family members and others will review what they have learned about the importance of maintaining healthy bodies and will think of things they need to do to improve the status of their health.
2. *Intellectual Competencies*—Each member of the family will discuss things they have learned from each other through the process of interaction in teaching and learning and will share ways in which they have stretched their brain-power to new dimensions of thinking and doing.
3. *Home and Family Relations*—Family members will share how they have grown and developed through interacting with each other.
4. *Social and Cultural Values*—Recognizing diversity in social and cultural values in society, family members will discuss their beliefs and communicate their objectives for orchestrating social and cultural values in the daily activities.
5. *Spiritual and Ethical Beliefs*—Inner-winning spirits of all family members will be cultivated to set and achieve standards of abiding faith in each other and demonstrations of correct choices for practicing right ways for bringing out the *best* in self and others.
6. *Career Development*—Family members will observe different careers and study about numerous careers in books. Advantages and disadvantages of each career should be

discussed and choice of careers should be made after pros and cons have been assessed.
7. *Financial Security*—Weekly discussions of economic security should be held by family members and other caretakers. The adage "a penny saved is a penny earned" should be explained and practiced. Exercises in budgeting should be a part of long and short-range plans. Income and expenditures should be discussed to ensure that everyone understands the importance of saving more than what they spend.

Budgeting and saving should be a part of the weekly process. Lesson plans should be made to include all aspects of healthy bodies, healthy minds, and healthy souls for coping with challenges.

The Power of the Family: Strength, Comfort, and Healing by Dr. Paul Pearsall is an impressive book that has a case study of five families and how they were empowered to solve their problems through his ten prescriptions for a healthy family. Included were family rituals, understanding how to practice resiliency, conflict resolution, reconciliation, problem-solving, unity, sharing family history, unconditional love, and celebration. Pearsall defines *family reunion* as: "The ability to draw more strongly together through awareness of the power of the family and an energy for life and loving, derived through a common faith in the spiritual strength of the family."[60]

Interacting at home, at school, and in the community continues to have positive outcomes for success in life as evidenced in several research studies. An example is the Follow Through Parent Education Model developed by Ira J. Gordon. Gordon emphasized the involvement of parents as partners in the educational process.[61] This study has been replicated with emphasis on building effective home, school, and community relationships. Gordon and his associates stated: "The changes in our society and in our schools challenge us to find new pathways back to our roots, new ways to tie together the two most formative learning centers for the child: home and school."[62]

Home Learning Activity

INTERACT FOR POSITIVE OUTCOMES

Hold family meetings to:

- Develop job descriptions for each family member from preschoolers to adults.
- Assess the effectiveness of job performances on a weekly basis.
- Engage in making family budgets that will encourage saving.
- Utilize teamwork in buying groceries and other items. (Look for sales.)
- Develop nutritional menus from advertisements in newspapers et. al. to determine the least expensive items.
- Make a list of favorite foods of each family member. Include at least one in the weekly diet.
- Play stock market games. Choose favorite stocks and observe the growth to see which member gained or lost the most on a monthly basis.
- Plan special celebrations for the family weekly meetings. Example: visit the library, museum, place of worship, and other places of interest.
- Make family booklets on what each member liked or disliked about each trip. Make illustrations or find appropriate pictures to cut out and paste in the booklets.
- Label the pictures of each place visited. Alphabetize and count them to build word and number recognition.
- Share the booklets with visiting friends.
- Make up stories and dramatize them to show how teamwork will have positive outcomes.

Chapter Seventeen

OPEN DOORS TO DIVERSITY

Roget's Thesaurus provides several synonyms for the word *diversity*: "difference; variance; heterogeneity, variety and assortment." One sure statement we can make is that we have similarities and we have differences. This is quite evident in our homes. This presents an even more important reason for the need to establish a strong homemade character education program.

Within the walls of our home exists human beings who act and react differently, have different tastes for food, favorite television programs, like different pastimes such as reading, watching television, working on the computer, listening to music, playing music or creating music, exercising, gardening, sleeping, and the list can go on and on. Diversity is alive and well within our homes.

Even though we are diverse in our daily living, we must still respect others. Opening doors to diversity is a great way of accentuating our character traits. Visualize the barrier we are attempting to convey in this chapter:

> Imagine a closed door. You are on one side and another human being is on the other. The only knowledge you have is that there is another person on the other side of the door. Is your curiosity escalating? Why of course it is! Your knowledge of what he or she is like is extremely limited. You can draw all kinds of conclusions. But until you see that person and have an opportunity to interact with him or her, conclusions are unfounded.

Opening the door to diversity provides a wealth of opportunities. First, once the door is opened, you can see the person on the other side. Second, opening the door gives both an opportunity to exercise one of the most beneficial gifts to humanity—communication. The two of you begin to talk with each other. The conversation helps to shed light on how you are alike and how you are different.

Opening the door welcomes communication. This is what we must do in order to understand each other. If we can get to the point of communicating with each other, more than likely we will begin to respect each other, become more considerate of each other, and care about the feelings of others.

Think of a situation in your home that presents a family conflict. Is it that of a family member staying in the bathroom for a long period of time? Could it be preparing a delicious meal, but no one has time to gather around the table and feast together? Think of ways family members can bring these issues to the forefront and lessen the conflicts. One person may enjoy staying in the bathroom and reading. If we are able and willing to talk with each other and express our feelings, it could lead to solving the problem surrounding personal differences.

Diversity does not always cause conflicts. Quite often it is different ways, ideas, and approaches coming together which helps to achieve a goal. Again, communication is the primary tool to express various ideas and approaches. As communication between participants takes place, a higher level of understanding becomes evident. Opening the door to diversity opens windows of conversation, understanding, respect, honesty, and consideration.

If we can open the door to diversity in our homes, that open door will extend into the schools, into the community, and wherever we go. Allowing that door to remain closed limits understanding, consideration, respect, and honesty and stifles communication. The ability to communicate with each other in our home is vital to the making and maintenance of a strong character education program.

Again, visualize the closed door we spoke of earlier. Do you think you have grown as a human being by opening the door and allowing a dialogue to take place? What has opening the door accomplished in your eyesight? Let us now look at a few possibilities. Opening the door provides an opportunity for one to see who is on the other side, sets the stage for questions as well as answers, and allows for both viewpoints to be expressed

We are surrounded daily by diversity of one sort or another. We may agree or disagree. But the fact of the matter remains, we live in a world where people have different opinions, ideas, likes, dislikes, cultures, and traditions. Think positively and think about the good things which can be derived from diversity. Visualize a huge natural field of flowers. Humans have not been given the opportunity to plant or transplant any flower into this massive area of flowers, blossoms, and beautiful foliage. Each flower is different. There are different colors, sizes, and shapes. But it takes each individual flower to add to the beauty, distinctiveness, and charm of this massive garden.

The distinctiveness of each flower carries a special beauty. If all flowers in this garden were of the same color, type, and size, the beauty of the whole would be greatly diminished. As you continue to observe this garden, you will see that each flower has its own unique beauty but seems to respect the space and beauty of other surrounding flowers.

As you work together as a family to enhance your character education program, please keep this point in mind. Open the door to diversity within your home. Give each family member an opportunity to communicate, evaluate, and come together to make the final decision. Also keep in mind that there are some decisions that you as adults must make. This should be understood in your home environment. But there are also opportunities where each family member can and should be heard.

Home Learning Activity

Open the Door to Diversity

Think of family situations that have resulted in a positive outcome because family members expressed different ideas, and a solution resulted in the compilation of everybody's input. Many times different ideas coming together can give rise to a different but workable outcome.

Chapter Eighteen

Nurture Success in the Journey of Life

Nourishment of mind, body, and soul is an ongoing process. It begins with conception and extends throughout human existence as we cope with challenges to our survival. Stages of development on the journey are enriched by a support system of caring, concerned, and positive reinforcers who keep lights of peaceful faith, stupendous hope for high achievement, and requited love ablaze.

Soothing music of encouragement builds bridges which withstand obstacles and adversities on the journey. Primary focus on nurturing will foster in each individual an "I can" attitude that will help them realize their fondest dreams.

Positive thinking leads to achievement of goals and objectives. People with a healthy self-esteem will be well-adjusted travelers on the tour of life. Hopefully, the encouragement in this book will help you achieve your desired goals as you journey towards character development.

Our goal for nurturing success on the journey of life must be couched with faith, hope, and unconditional love for achievement of desired outcomes of the trip and attainment of group and individual satisfaction.

We believe that mind, body, and soul must be committed to making character education a reality that will enhance the quality of life for all participants. Concerted efforts of all family members will provide necessary nurturing for developing maximum support systems.

Here are our suggestions for ensuring success in the pursuit of excellence:

N   *Navigate the course* for life's journey by naming your goals.

U   *Understand the rules* of desired behavior and the need to have conduct guidelines.

R   *Reward success* for conforming to accepted standards of conduct in home, school, the workplace, and community.

T   *Teach and learn* as a family of caregivers and caretakers traveling together with unity of purpose on a successful journey.

U   *Undergird the foundation of peace* with continuous building of self-acceptance, self-control, self-respect, self-confidence, and self-worth.

R   *Respond to needs and fill them.*

E   *Expect the best* from each family member on your journey of success.

S   *Search for ways to improve* the journey of life by reviewing plans and strategies that will empower each traveler to achieve the stated goals.

U   *Underline areas of strengths* that have been accomplished as well as those that need improvement.

C   *Change courses of travel* when adversities and obstacles are encountered on the trip.

C   *Communicate needs and interests* of each participant on the journey of success.

E   *Energize each traveler* with positive affirmations to stay focused on purpose.

S   *Set challenging goals* to be achieved on both a short and long-range basis.

S   *Sap negative thoughts and actions* that impede progress on the pathway to success.

HOME LEARNING ACTIVITY

NURTURE SUCCESS ON THE JOURNEY OF LIFE

Plan imaginary trips that each family member desires to take. List the name of the place to be visited. Find it on the map and search for other information about it.

1. Indicate the city, town, state, and country.

_____
_____
_____
_____

2. What are some of its important human and material resources?

_____
_____
_____
_____

3. What is the distance from your home to the place to be visited?

_____
_____
_____
_____

4. What is the climate in each season?

_____
_____
_____
_____

5. What ways will you travel to get there? How long will it take?

_____
_____
_____
_____

6. How long will you stay at this place?

_____
_____
_____
_____

7. How much money will be needed for:

Food _____
Housing _____
Recreation _____
Other _____

8. Describe what you will do each day.

_____
_____
_____
_____
_____
_____
_____
_____
_____

9. What will you learn from visiting this place that will increase your achievement or standards of learning?

_____
_____
_____
_____
_____
_____
_____
_____
_____

Write a short letter to the chamber of commerce in the place you desire to visit and ask for brochures and other materials that will help you increase your understanding of the place, people, and activities.

Epilogue

Through our reflection on a wide array of theories and practices, it is clear that character education is an integral part of teaching and learning. As you move forward with your own model of character education, keep the following affirmations in mind. We hope they will help you embrace character education and implement character-building activities into your daily life.

- Portray moral excellence at home, school, the workplace, and in community activities.
- Utilize professional standards of conduct in actions and interactions.
- When you plan for behavior improvement, change courses if satisfaction is not achieved.
- Faith, hope, and unconditional love must be a part of daily activities.
- Expect the best and you'll get the best in most situations.
- Build hope in planning and implementing activities.
- Identify problems and utilize techniques to find the best possible solutions.
- Be caring, concerned, and committed to achieving excellence from teaching/learning experiences.
- Practice energizing self and others for optimum results.
- Communicate with all family members and others on a two-way basis.
- Think before you speak and try to react in positive ways.
- Avoid negative criticisms and put-downs.
- Learn something new every day and find ways to apply the knowledge.
- Practice sharing and caring which are bridge-builders of faith.
- Plan ways to promote character education and work your plan on a daily basis.
- Take time to enjoy family life and serve as role models. Others will replicate your actions.
- Demonstrate unconditional love for all people and make the pathways of life glow with a positive mental attitude.

NOTES

1. David T. Kearns and Denis P. Doyle, *Winning the Brain Race* (San Francisco: ICS Press, 1988), 12.

2. Marva Collins and Civia Tamarkin, *Marva Collins' Way: Any Child Can Be a Real Achiever* (Los Angeles: J. P. Tarcher, 1990), 51–52.

3. Celia Decker, *Children: The Early Years* (South Holland, Ill.: Goodheart-Wilcox Co., 1990), 28.

4. Sue Spayh Riley, *How to Generate Values in Young Children* (Newport Beach, Calif.: The New South Co., 1979), 17.

5. Charles Schaefer, *How to Influence Children: A Handbook of Practical Parenting Skills* (New York: Van Nostrand Reinhold, 1982), 114–16.

6. James E. Shaw, *Jack and Jill, Why They Kill: Saving Our Children, Saving Ourselves* (Seattle, Wash.: Onjinjinkta Publishing, 2000), 7–8.

7. Amy Eckman, *Learning on the Home Front* (Association for Supervision and Curriculum Development Curriculum Update: Spring 2001), 7.

8. William J. Bennett, *The Book of Virtues* (New York: Simon & Schuster, 1993), 528.

9. Helen R. LeGette, *Parents, Kids and Character: 21 Strategies to Help Your Child Develop Good Character* (Chapel Hill, N.C.: Character Development Publishers [Center for Youth Issues], 1998), 1.

10. Bennett, *The Book of Virtues*, 11.

11. Shaw, *Jack and Jill, Why They Kill*, 24.

12. LeGette, *Parents, Kids, and Character*, 1.

13. James Comer, *Maggie's American Dream.* (New York: New American Library, 1988), 227.

14. U.S. Senator John McCain, "Commencement Speech," *Richmond Times Dispatch*, May 19, 2001.

15. William Menninger, "Dec. 19, 1979," in *Daily Thoughts for School Administrators*, ed. Joseph F. Halloran. (Reading, Mass.: Principals' Information and Resource Center, 1979).

16. Charles Garfield, *Peak Performers: The New Heroes of American Business* (New York: William Monroe & Co., 1986), 269.

17. John W. Gardner, "March 12, 1979," in *Daily Thoughts for School Administrators*, ed. Joseph F. Halloran. (Reading, Mass.: Principals' Information and Resource Center, 1979).

18. Frank Lloyd Wright, "May 27, 1979," in *Daily Thoughts for School Administrators*, ed. Joseph F. Halloran. (Reading, Mass.: Principals' Information and Resource Center, 1979).

19. Nathan M. Pusey, "Sept. 13, 1979," in *Daily Thoughts for School Administrators*, ed. Joseph F. Halloran. (Reading, Mass.: Principals' Information and Resource Center, 1979).

20. Galileo Galilei, "Oct. 8, 1979," in *Daily Thoughts for School Administrators*, ed. Joseph F. Halloran. (Reading, Mass.: Principals' Information and Resource Center, 1979).

21. Karl Menninger, "Oct. 30, 1979," in *Daily Thoughts for School Administrators*, ed. Joseph F. Halloran. (Reading, Mass.: Principals' Information and Resource Center, 1979).

22. Horace Mann, "Nov. 18, 1979," in *Daily Thoughts for School Administrators*, ed. Joseph F. Halloran. (Reading, Mass.: Principals' Information and Resource Center, 1979).

23. John Lubbock, "Jan 16, 1979," in *Daily Thoughts for School Administrators*, ed. Joseph F. Halloran. (Reading, Mass.: Principals' Information and Resource Center, 1979).

24. John Dewey, "Dec. 29, 1979," in *Daily Thoughts for School Administrators*, ed. Joseph F. Halloran. (Reading, Mass.: Principals' Information and Resource Center, 1979).

25. Joseph Epstein, *Masters: Portraits of Great Teachers* (New York: Basic Books, 1981), xii.

26. Locke E. Bowman, *Teaching Today* (Philadephia: The Westminster Press, 1980), 22.

27. Walter B. Barbe, *Growing Up Learning: The Key to Your Child's Potential* (Washington, D.C.: Acropolis Books, Ltd., 1985), 195.

28. LeGette, *Parents, Kids, and Character*, 4.

29. Ibid.

30. Ron Hutchcraft, *Five Needs Your Child **Must** Have Met at Home* (Grand Rapids: Zondervan, 1994), 29.

31. Dorothy Rich, *What Do We Say? What Do We Do?: Vital Solutions for Children's Educational Success* (New York: Tor Books, 1997), 76.

32. Donald Walton, *Are You Communicating? You Can't Manage Without It* (New York: McGraw-Hill, 1989), 69–70.

33. Steven R. Mamchak and P. Susan Mamchak, *School Administrators Public Speaking Portfolio* (West Nyack, N.Y.: Parker Publishing, 1983), 138.

34. Greg H. Quinn, *365 Meditations for Teachers* (New York: Scholastic, 1995).

35. Zelda Maggart and Miles V. Zintz, *The Reading Process: The Teacher and the Learner* (Dubuque, Iowa: W. C. Brown Co. Publishers, 1992), 78.

36. William Lampton, *The Complete Communicator* (Franklin, Tenn.: Hillsboro Press, 1999), 21.

37. Leo Buscaglia, *Living, Loving and Learning* (New York: Fawcett, 1982), 194.

38. LeGette, *Parents, Kids, and Character*, 2.

39. Jeanne M. Machado and Helen C. Meyer, *Early Childhood Practicum Guide* (New York: Delmar, 1984), 82.

40. Ronald G. Slaby, *Early Violence Prevention: Tools for Teachers of Young Children* (Washington, D.C.: National Association for the Education of Young Children, 1995), 81, 96.

41. Jack McGuire with Philadelphia Child Guidance Center, *Your Child's Emotional Health* (New York: Macmillan, 1993), 207.

42. Linda Eyre and Richard Eyre, *Steps to a Strong Family* (New York: Simon & Schuster, 1994), 219.

43. Denise Lang, *Family Harmony: Coping with Your Challenging Relatives* (New York: Prentice-Hall, 1990), 247.

44. Myrna Schure, *I Can Problem Solve: Raising a Thinking Preteen* (New York: Henry Holt, 2000), 4–5.

45. Ibid., 28.

46. Jeannette Shalov, *You Can Say No to Your Teenager and Other Strategies for Effective Parenting in the 1990s* (Reading, Mass.: Addison-Wesley, 1991), 4.

47. Ibid., 36.

48. Ibid., 58–59.

49. Harris Clemes and R. Bean, *Self-Esteem: The Key to Your Child's Well-Being* (New York: G. P. Putnams Sons, 1981), 216.

50. Ibid., 229–30.

51. LeGette, *Parents, Kids, and Character*, 2.

52. Shaw, *Jack and Jill, Why They Kill*, 225.

53. Quinn, *365 Meditations*, 199.

54. Marsha Sinetar, *Developing a 21st Century Mind* (New York: Ballantine Books, 1991), 199.

55. Robert Anthony, *The Ultimate Secrets of Self-Confidence* (New York: Berkley Books, 1984), 131–32.

56. Jacob Braude, *Complete Speakers and Toastmasters Library* (Englewood Cliffs, N.J.: Prentice-Hall, 1965), 285.

57. Ibid., 187.

58. Jacob M. Braude, *Lifetime Speakers Encyclopedia Volume 1.* (Englewood Cliffs, N.J.: Prentice-Hall, 1962), 487.

59. Jacob M. Braude, *Speakers Deskbook of Quips, Quotes and Anecdotes.* (Englewood Cliffs, N.J.: Prentice-Hall, 1963), 197.

60. Paul Pearsall, *The Power of the Family: Strength, Comfort, and Healing* (New York: Doubleday, 1990), 320.

61. Ira J. Gordon, "The Parent Education Follow Through Program." (A project funded under USDE grant number G00-77-01691), (Chapel Hill, N.C.: July 1977), 3.

62. Ira J. Gordon, ed. *Building Effective Home-School Relationships* (Boston, Mass.: Allyn and Bacon, 1976), 2.

Bibliography

Anthony, Robert. *The Ultimate Secrets of Self-Confidence.* New York: Berkley Books, 1984.

Armington, David. *The Living Classroom.* Washington, D.C.: National Association for the Education of Young Children, 1997.

Barbe, Walter B. *Growing Up Learning: The Key to Your Child's Potential.* Washington, D.C.: Acropolis Books Ltd., 1985.

Bennett, William J. *The Book of Virtues.* New York: Simon & Schuster, 1993.

Bowman, Locke E. *Teaching Today.* Philadelphia: The Westminster Press, 1980.

Braude, Jacob M., ed. *Complete Speakers and Toastmasters Library.* Englewood Cliffs, N.J.: Prentice-Hall, 1965.

———. *Lifetime Speakers Encyclopedia Volume 1.* Englewood Cliffs, N.J.: Prentice-Hall, 1962.

———. *Speakers Deskbook of Quips, Quotes, and Anecdotes.* Englewood Cliffs, N.J.: Prentice-Hall, 1963.

Buscaglia, Leo. *Living, Loving and Learning.* New York: Fawcett, 1982.

Clemes, Harris and R. Bean. *Self-Esteem: The Key to Your Child's Well-Being.* New York: G. P. Putnams Sons, 1981.

Comer, James. *Maggie's American Dream.* New York: New American Library, 1988.

Decker, Celia. *Children: The Early Years.* South Holland, Ill.: Goodheart-Wilcox Co., 1990.

Eckman, Amy, *Learning on the Homefront: Engaging Parents in the Learning Process.* Association for Supervision and Curriculum Development Curriculum Update, Spring 2001.

Epstein, Joseph. *Masters: Portraits of Great Teachers.* New York: Basic Books, 1981.

Eyre, Linda and Richard Eyre. *Steps to a Strong Family.* New York: Simon & Schuster, 1994.

Garfield, Charles. *Peak Performers: The New Heroes of American Business.* New York: William Monroe & Co., 1986.

Gordon, Ira J., and others. *Building Effective Home-School Relationships.* Boston: Allyn and Bacon, 1976.

Halloran, Joseph F., ed. *Daily Thoughts for School Administrators.* Reading, Mass.: Principal's Information and Research Center, 1979.

Hutchcraft, Ron. *Five Needs Your Child **Must** Have Met at Home.* Grand Rapids: Zondervan, 1994.

Kearns, David T. and Denis P. Doyle. *Winning the Brain Race: A Bold Plan to Make Our Schools Competitive.* San Francisco, Calif.: ICS Press, 1988.

Lampton, William. *The Complete Communicator.* Franklin, Tenn.: Hillsboro Press, 1999.

Lang, Denise. *Family Harmony: Coping with Your Challenging Relatives.* New York: Prentice-Hall, 1990.

LeGette, Helen R. *Parents, Kids and Character: 21 Strategies to Help Your Child Develop Good Character.* Chapel Hill, N.C.: Character Development Publishers, (Center for Youth Issues), 1998.

Machado, Jeanne M. and Helen C. Meyer. *Early Childhood Practicum Guide.* New York: Delmar, 1984.

Mackay, Harvey. *Dig Your Well Before You Are Thirsty.* New York: Doubleday, 1991.

Maggart, Zelda and Miles V. Zintz. *The Reading Process: The Teacher and the Learner.* Dubuque, Iowa: W. C. Brown Co. Publishers, 1992.

Mamchak, Steven R. and P. Susan Mamchak. *School Administrators Public Speaking Portfolio*. West Nyack, N.Y.: Parker Publishing, 1983.

McGuire, Jack with Philadelphia Child Guidance Center. *Your Child's Emotional Health*. New York: Macmillan, 1993.

Pearsall, Paul. *The Power of the Family*. New York: Doubleday, 1990.

Quinn, Greg H., ed. *365 Meditations for Teachers*. New York: Scholastic, 1995.

Rich, Dorothy. *What Do We Say? What Do We Do?: Vital Solutions for Children's Educational Success*. New York: Tor Books, 1997.

Riley, Sue Spayh. *How to Generate Values in Young Children*. Newport Beach, Calif.: The New South Co., 1979.

Schaefer, Charles. *How to Influence Children: A Handbook of Practical Parenting Skills*. New York: Van Nostrand Reinhold, 1978.

Schloff, Laure and Marcia Yudkin. *Smart Speaking: Sixty Second Strategies*. New York: Henry Holt, 1991.

Schure, Myrna. *I Can Problem Solve: Raising a Thinking Preteen*. New York: Henry Holt, 2000.

Shalov, Jeannette et. al. *You Can Say No to Your Teenager and Other Strategies for Effective Parenting in the 1990s*. Reading, Mass.: Addison-Wesley, 1991.

Shaw, James E. *Jack and Jill, Why They Kill: Saving Our Children, Saving Ourselves*. Seattle, Wash.: Onjinjinkta Publishing, 2000.

Sinetar, Marsha. *Developing a 21st Century Mind*. New York: Ballantine Books, 1991.

Slaby, Ronald G. et. al. *Early Violence Prevention: Tools for Teachers of Young Children*. Washington, D.C.: National Association for the Education of Young Children, 1995.

Walton, Donald. *Are You Communicating? You Can't Manage Without It*. New York: McGraw-Hill, 1989.

About the Authors

VIRGIE M. BINFORD is an educational consultant, motivational speaker, and workshop facilitator. She serves on the executive board of directors of the National Council on Self-Esteem. A graduate of Virginia State University, Binford earned her bachelor and master's degrees in elementary education before earning her doctorate at Virginia Tech. She has studied at Columbia University and has furthered her education at the University of Virginia and in international studies. Binford served Richmond Public Schools as a teacher, supervisor, and director of various early-childhood and elementary-education programs, and she has taught at Virginia Union University and J. Sargeant Reynolds Community College. She is actively involved in civic, church, and educational organizations, including the National Coalition of 100 Black Women, All Souls Presbyterian Church, and Pi Lambda Theta International Honor Society in Education.

RONA LEACH is a director for her school system in Robeson County, North Carolina. She was raised as the only child of her parents, the late Ranzie and Sarah Leach. Rona earned her bachelor of arts degree from St. Andrews Presbyterian College, two masters degrees from North Carolina A&T State University, and her doctorate in educational leadership from Nova University in Fort Lauderdale, Florida. She has served as a middle school teacher, assistant principal, principal of several middle and junior high schools, and taught several courses through the community college. Working with children extends beyond her job and into her church and community. She has a passion for helping others by giving back to the world what has been given to her. Her goal is to continue helping others through her writing of children's books.